Thinking Critically: Medical Marijuana

Bonnie Szumski and Jill Karson

San Diego, CA

ReferencePoint
Press®

About the Author

Bonnie Szumski has been an editor and author of nonfiction books for over twenty-five years. Jill Karson has been a writer and editor of nonfiction books for young adults for fifteen years.

© 2014 ReferencePoint Press, Inc.
Printed in the United States

For more information, contact:
ReferencePoint Press, Inc.
PO Box 27779
San Diego, CA 92198
www. ReferencePointPress.com

Cover credit: Thinkstock Images
Thinkstock Images: 9
Steve Zmina: 16, 21, 30, 37, 42, 49, 55, 62

LIBRARY OF CONGRESS CATALOGING-IN-PUBLICATION DATA

Szumski, Bonnie, 1958-
  Thinking critically. Medical marijuana / by Bonnie Szumski and Jill Karson.
    pages cm. -- (Thinking critically series)
  Includes bibliographical references and index.
  ISBN-13: 978-1-60152-582-6 (hardback)
  ISBN-10: 1-60152-582-6 (hardback)
  1. Marijuana--Therapeutic use. 2. Marijuana--United States. 3. Marijuana--Law and legislation--United States. I. Karson, Jill. II. Title. III. Title: Medical marijuana.
  RM666.C266S983 2013
  615.7'827--dc23
                                                                                    2012047796

Contents

Foreword   4

Overview: Medical Marijuana   6

Chapter One: Is Medical Marijuana Effective Medicine?

The Debate at a Glance   12

Medical Marijuana Is Effective Medicine   13

Medical Marijuana Is Not Effective Medicine   19

Chapter Two: Is Medical Marijuana Safe?

The Debate at a Glance   26

Medical Marijuana Is Safe   27

Medical Marijuana Is Not Safe   33

Chapter Three: Should Medical Marijuana Be Legalized?

The Debate at a Glance   39

Medical Marijuana Should Not Be Legalized   40

Medical Marijuana Should Be Legalized   46

Chapter Four: Can States Adequately Regulate Medical Marijuana?

The Debate at a Glance   52

States Cannot Adequately Regulate Medical Marijuana   53

States Can Adequately Regulate Medical Marijuana   59

Source Notes   65

Medical Marijuana Facts   70

Related Organizations and Websites   72

For Further Research   76

Index   78

Foreword

"Literacy is the most basic currency of the knowledge economy we're living in today." Barack Obama (at the time a senator from Illinois) spoke these words during a 2005 speech before the American Library Association. One question raised by this statement is: What does it mean to be a literate person in the twenty-first century?

E.D. Hirsch Jr., author of *Cultural Literacy: What Every American Needs to Know*, answers the question this way: "To be culturally literate is to possess the basic information needed to thrive in the modern world. The breadth of the information is great, extending over the major domains of human activity from sports to science."

But literacy in the twenty-first century goes beyond the accumulation of knowledge gained through study and experience and expanded over time. Now more than ever literacy requires the ability to sift through and evaluate vast amounts of information and, as the authors of the Common Core State Standards state, to "demonstrate the cogent reasoning and use of evidence that is essential to both private deliberation and responsible citizenship in a democratic republic."

The Thinking Critically series challenges students to become discerning readers, to think independently, and to engage and develop their skills as critical thinkers. Through a narrative-driven, pro/con format, the series introduces students to the complex issues that dominate public discourse—topics such as gun control and violence, social networking, and medical marijuana. All chapters revolve around a single, pointed question such as Can Stronger Gun Control Measures Prevent Mass Shootings?, or Does Social Networking Benefit Society?, or Should Medical Marijuana Be Legalized? This inquiry-based approach introduces student researchers to core issues and concerns on a given topic. Each chapter includes one part that argues the affirmative and one part that argues the negative—all written by a single author. With the single-author format the predominant arguments for and against an issue can be synthesized into clear, accessible discussions supported by details and evidence including relevant facts, direct quotes, current examples, and statistical illustrations. All volumes include focus questions to guide students as they read each pro/con discussion, a list of key facts, and an annotated list of related organizations and websites for conducting further research.

The authors of the Common Core State Standards have set out the particular qualities that a literate person in the twenty-first century must have. These include the ability to think independently, establish a base of knowledge across a wide range of subjects, engage in open-minded but discerning reading and listening, know how to use and evaluate evidence, and appreciate and understand diverse perspectives. The new Thinking Critically series supports these goals by providing a solid introduction to the study of pro/con issues.

Medical Marijuana

Without a doubt, attitudes are changing toward the issue of medical marijuana. By the end of 2012, eighteen states had legalized it. A 2010 Pew
Research poll found that 73 percent of the public favor "their state allowing the sale and use of marijuana for medical purposes, if it is prescribed
by a doctor."[1] More people have become convinced that marijuana is a
medical, not a legal, issue and that it should be offered as a treatment
option for those who struggle with pain, nausea, and crippling diseases.
People's attitudes, for the most part, have been changed by the stories of
people like Gustin L. Reichbach. Until he was diagnosed in 2009 with
stage 3 pancreatic cancer, Reichbach had served as a justice of the New
York Supreme Court. In that capacity, he had upheld state laws that made
many drugs, including medical marijuana, illegal.

Reichbach, who died in 2012, had used medical marijuana to stave
off the nausea and pain that accompanied aggressive rounds of chemotherapy. As both a justice professional and cancer patient, he had a
unique view on the need for legalization of medical marijuana. In direct
opposition to many of his friends, who believed that publicly supporting
medical marijuana would jeopardize his career, Reichbach believed that
he had a moral duty to speak out. In a 2012 editorial in the *New York
Times,* he wrote:

> This is not a law-and-order issue; it is a medical and a human
> rights issue. Being a patient at Memorial Sloan Kettering Can-
> cer Center, I am receiving the absolute gold standard of medical
> care. But doctors cannot be expected to do what the law prohib-
> its, even when it is in the best interests of their patients. When

palliative care is understood as a fundamental human and medical right, marijuana for medical use should be beyond controversy. . . .

It is another heartbreaking aporia [contradiction] in the world of cancer that the one drug that gives us relief without deleterious side effects remains classified as a narcotic with no medicinal value. . . .

I feel obliged to speak out as both a judge and a cancer patient suffering with a fatal disease. . . . Medical science has not yet found a cure, but it is barbaric to deny us access to one substance that has proved to ameliorate our suffering.[2]

Voters Speak

Such plaintive cries for treatment are hard to ignore. In many states voters have turned to the polls to voice their support for ill and suffering patients to have the right to use marijuana. Yet although the public thinks marijuana is a legitimate treatment, the federal government does not agree. The federal government's position, ironically, hampers researchers who want to perform studies to settle the issue. Marijuana currently has a schedule 1 drug classification, which ranks it in the same class as heroin and LSD—considered to have no medical use and to have a high potential for abuse. Despite numerous petitions to change marijuana's status, including as recently as 2011, the federal government has not budged. This has left pharmaceutical companies that want to develop products with marijuana in a catch-22 situation. To study marijuana, such labs must have their research approved by the federal government in order to purchase the substance legally. But the federal government makes it virtually impossible to obtain such permission.

The federal government has not wavered on its position on marijuana. This has not been the case in a number of states where voters have chosen to legalize marijuana. Once a marijuana law is passed, it is up to the individual state to develop a process of regulating medical marijuana's production, distribution, and use while adhering to federal law. This, however, has proven difficult for states to accomplish. Many, such as California, have found it nearly impossible to satisfy both the requirements of the federal government and the desires of the public.

A Clash Between State and Federal Laws

So although the public's attitude has changed toward marijuana as its medical value has gained acceptance, the federal government's position has not changed. This has left states and patients in legal limbo. In California, for example, a dispensary must be able to prove that it obtained its marijuana in-state and only from state-approved growers. Hundreds of California dispensaries have been closed for not complying with state laws such as this one even though growers and dispensaries have argued successfully in court that they were operating within state guidelines.

Time magazine writer Michael Scherer describes the battleground between the federal and state governments as boiling down to a lack of trust: "Federal prosecutors have lost faith in the ability of state and local officials to control a booming commercial industry for a drug that is still illegal to grow, possess or sell under federal law. As a result, a once broad exemption from prosecution for medical marijuana providers in states where it is legal has been narrowed to a tiny one."[3]

States Increase Regulation of Marijuana

States that have legalized medical marijuana have been working overtime to increase oversight and regulation of the drug. Colorado and Connecticut, for example, have laws in place for monitoring and regulating every part of the marijuana business. Only certain growing operations are licensed by the state, every plant is tagged and inspected, and growers can only sell and dispense marijuana to licensed distributors. Connecticut also has tough restrictions on who is allowed to obtain a marijuana prescription. Only eleven medical conditions, including AIDS, glaucoma, Parkinson's disease, and multiple sclerosis, are sanctioned by the state. To obtain a prescription, a patient's doctor must register him or her with

Although voters in many states have given their support to legalization of marijuana for medical purposes, the federal government still classifies marijuana as a dangerous and addictive substance with no medical benefits. These conflicting views ensure continued debate on this volatile topic.

the Department of Consumer Protection and submit documentation to show that the individual qualifies for the program. Marijuana use is prohibited in vehicles, workplaces, schools, dormitories, and all public places, and it cannot be used in front of anyone under the age of eighteen. Violation of any of these stipulations makes the patient vulnerable to prosecution.

Colorado and Connecticut are trying to learn from—and avoid—the problems that have occurred in California. In that state, growers and dispensaries have found loopholes to be able to operate in opposition to California's marijuana law. The proliferation of hundreds of dispensaries has intensified the debate in California. Such dispensaries operate on virtually every downtown street corner and have led many neighbors and businesses in such areas to seek zoning laws to have them removed. The sheer numbers of dispensaries in California have called into question whether they can all be serving people with legitimate medical issues. Since the federal government has stated that it will not tolerate recreational marijuana use, it has been particularly aggressive in shutting down California dispensaries—shutting down such places first, and having the burden of proof that they are legitimate fall on the side of the dispensary.

The Federal Government Maintains Its Stance

Observers point out, however, that no matter how rigorous state governance of marijuana is, federal law still prohibits the cultivation, distribution, and possession of marijuana. And the federal government, while avoiding prosecuting individuals, has been targeting marijuana businesses, using both the US Department of Justice and the Internal Revenue Service (IRS). Even businesses that comply with state laws are worried. Norton Arbelaez, cofounder of RiverRock, a Denver medical marijuana dispensary, says, "In any other business, if you fail, you file for bankruptcy and move on. If you fail in this business, you go to jail. . . . The one thing I can hold onto is complete compliance. The Colorado legal code is our only line of defense. It's the only way to show regulation is better than prohibition."[4]

As of 2012, however, such state compliance has not helped those in the marijuana industry. The federal government seems to find large facilities such as RiverRock particularly objectionable. President Barack Obama said in a *Rolling Stone* interview that "the only tension that's come up . . . is a murky area where you have large-scale commercial operations that may also be supplying medical marijuana users."[5] The government does not seem averse to using everything in its power to at least hassle, if not completely shut down, such operations. One of the least obvious is using the IRS to audit dispensaries by prosecuting them under a section of the federal tax code that prohibits companies from deducting expenses related to drug trafficking. The IRS has insisted that many of these operations owe millions of dollars in back taxes. In response, Steve DeAngelo, owner of Harborside Health Center in Oakland, California, has said that it is an "attempt to tax us out of existence." DeAngelo remarks that "no business in America could survive if all of its expense deductions were disallowed."[6]

In a nutshell then, the federal government, concerned that marijuana businesses are going beyond their purview and marketing to recreational users, continues to find ways to shut down growers and dispensaries. On the other hand, states are attempting to satisfy the public's mandate to offer patients valuable treatment by restricting and refining their regulations regarding marijuana. And yet the heart of the matter continues to be an impossible conundrum: how can any industry be regulated when it is legal in individual states but illegal in the nation? The final outcome remains to be seen. As San Francisco's district attorney, George Garcon, summarizes, "As a country we are being almost bipolar when it comes to drug policy."[7]

Chapter One

Is Medical Marijuana Effective Medicine?

Medical Marijuana Is Effective Medicine

- The medicinal benefits of marijuana are well documented by numerous studies.
- For some people, marijuana offers the best or only relief from pain and other ailments.
- Marijuana offers unlimited potential in many areas of medicine.

The Debate at a Glance

Medical Marijuana Is Not Effective Medicine

- In the absence of rigorous testing, the medicinal benefits of marijuana are unsubstantiated.
- Marijuana is no more helpful at alleviating glaucoma symptoms than conventional treatments.
- Serious side effects call into question marijuana's effectiveness in treating various medical conditions.

Marijuana Is Effective Medicine

"Marijuana is one of the safest therapeutically active substances known. No one has ever died from an overdose, and it has a wide variety of therapeutic applications."

Marijuana Policy Project, "The Need to Change State and Federal Law," August 2011. www.mpp.org.

Consider these questions as you read:

1. The author argues that marijuana is an effective medicine for several conditions. Should effectiveness be the main criterion used when legalizing a medicine? Why or why not?
2. While the author believes medical marijuana should be allowed, others argue it has not passed US Food and Drug Administration (FDA) safety tests. Do you think marijuana should be required to go through the FDA approval process? Why or why not?
3. After reading this viewpoint and the next one, which do you agree with? Why?

Editor's note: The discussion that follows presents common arguments made in support of this perspective, reinforced by facts, quotes, and examples taken from various sources.

Numerous studies prove that marijuana effectively treats many medical conditions, as well as alleviates pain and nausea. Thousands of people continue to suffer from conditions that could easily be alleviated with the use of marijuana, with fewer side effects than conventional treatments. Not allowing patients to use and doctors to prescribe marijuana is simple ignorance. In short, marijuana's therapeutic effects are well documented in three areas: its ability to inhibit pain, its ability to ameliorate nausea and spur appetite, and its ability to control muscle spasticity.

Pain

Because of its analgesic and anti-inflammatory properties, marijuana is widely used to relieve chronic pain related to a wide variety of conditions. Marijuana derives from the cannabis plant, which contains over 480 chemicals. Of these, 66 are cannabinoids. Cannabinoids are chemicals that also are produced by the human body. These cannabinoids attach themselves to the cannabinoid receptors that are found throughout the body—in the brain and other organs, the immune system, and other areas. This so-called endocannabinoid system is involved in regulating many body systems by turning certain functions off or on. Cannabinoids appear to help regulate appetite, movement, pain, memory, mood, immunity, inflammation, reproduction, and other bodily functions. Because marijuana also contains cannabinoids—more than 60 different kinds that may yield different properties—it can enhance the body's governance of these same functions. For example, tetrahydrocannabinol (THC) and other cannabinoids may turn off the body's pain receptors, resulting in a decrease in the severity of pain.

Millions of Americans suffer from chronic pain that is not alleviated by traditional medicines. Critics often charge that medical marijuana is not necessary to treat pain because abundant legal painkillers are already available. The issue, however, is that not all medications work for everyone. As the Marijuana Policy Project, an advocacy group, succinctly puts it: "Consider all the over-the-counter pain medications: aspirin, acetaminophen, ibuprofen, etc. We do not just determine which is 'best' and then ban all of the rest. Because patients are different, doctors must have the freedom to choose what works best for a particular patient. Why use a double standard for marijuana?"[8]

Some of the most promising results involving medical marijuana focus on neuropathic pain, which is the most difficult kind of pain to treat. This type of pain often results in a burning, painful hypersensitivity in the feet and legs and, less often, the hands and arms. Neuropathic pain results when the nervous system is damaged, usually from a trauma such as a stroke or an infection or from a disease such as multiple sclerosis, diabetes, or AIDS. Some of the most important research on pain has come out of the Center for Medicinal Cannabis Research (CMCR) at the University of California at San Diego. From 2001 to 2012 the center produced four completed studies—the first clinical trials of smoked marijuana in the United States in twenty years. These studies indicate that marijuana may indeed be useful in the treatment of pain.

Two of these studies focused on HIV patients. In 2007 a study on neuropathic pain related to HIV infection was published in the journal *Neurology*. In this study, smoked marijuana effectively relieved a painful nerve disorder that affects roughly 30 percent of HIV patients. Medications traditionally used for this type of pain do not work for all patients, may interfere with antiviral medications used to treat HIV, and may have debilitating side effects that make them unacceptable for some patients. Daniel Abrams, a professor of clinical medicine at the University of California at San Francisco, wrote about the study's conclusion: "Smoked cannabis was well tolerated and effectively relieved chronic neuropathic pain from HIV-associated sensory neuropathy. The findings are comparable to oral drugs used for chronic neuropathic pain."[9]

> "Consider all the over-the-counter pain medications: aspirin, acetaminophen, ibuprofen, etc. We do not just determine which is 'best' and then ban all of the rest. Because patients are different, doctors must have the freedom to choose what works best for a particular patient."[8]
>
> —Marijuana Policy Project, a marijuana advocacy group.

Nausea and Appetite Stimulation

In addition to pain management, medical marijuana has a well-documented, beneficial effect for people suffering from nausea and appetite loss. Two groups particularly affected by these symptoms are cancer patients undergoing chemotherapy and patients afflicted with HIV. Marijuana's ability to stimulate appetite is due to THC, the main psychoactive ingredient in marijuana, which stimulates the intestinal receptors in much the same way fatty foods do.

Scott Rozman, for example, was diagnosed with an aggressive form of cancer that required doctors to treat him with multiple rounds of

The Medical Benefits of Marijuana

When marijuana is smoked, its active ingredient, THC, travels to the brain. There it attaches to cannabinoid receptors. Once attached, the THC produces effects that benefit people who are experiencing serious pain, nausea, loss of appetite, and other ailments.

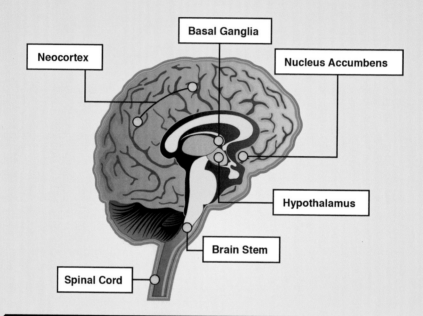

Brain Structure	Regulates	The Effect on User
Basal Ganglia	Planning/starting a movement	Slowed reaction time
Brain Stem	Information between brain and spinal column	Antinausea effects
Hypothalamus	Eating, sexual behavior	Increased appetite
Neocortex	Complex thinking, feeling, and movement	Altered thinking, judgment, and sensation
Nucleus Accumbens	Motivation and reward	Euphoria (feeling good)
Spinal Cord	Transmission of information between body and brain	Altered pain sensitivity

Source: "The Science of the Endocannaboid System: How THC Affects the Brain and Body," Scholastic.com, 2011. www.scholastic.com.

chemotherapy directed at the middle of his chest. The intensity of the treatment caused Rozman to vomit forty to fifty times a day. He lost sixty pounds in two months and was so weak the doctors feared he would not be able to complete the treatment. His doctors prescribed marijuana in hopes that he would be able to keep the nausea and vomiting at bay. The treatment worked—Rozman was able to eat, gain weight, and be calmer and more relaxed during the grueling chemotherapy sessions. Many cancer patients report similar results from using the drug.

With their immune systems deeply compromised and the need to maintain a healthy weight nearly impossible, many cancer patients and HIV sufferers have a difficult time eating because of debilitating nausea. Nausea is so severe that taking traditional medications to treat it may also cause cancer patients to vomit. Marijuana, on the other hand, stimulates the appetite and dulls the impulse to vomit. A review of studies published from 2000 to 2009 by the American Medical Association concluded that marijuana improved appetite and calorie intake in cancer patients undergoing chemotherapy.

Marijuana is so effective at safely relieving nausea that some pregnant women use it to alleviate severe morning sickness. During pregnancy some women become so severely nauseated that they lose weight and become dehydrated and malnourished, which is extremely dangerous to the developing fetus. Erin Hildebrandt explains how she used marijuana to counter the severe nausea and vomiting that made her first pregnancy high risk. When confronted with the same symptoms during her second pregnancy, she chose marijuana. "I know that using marijuana saved us both from many of the terrible dangers associated with malnutrition in pregnancy."[10]

Seizures and Spasticity

Marijuana has many uses. It relieves pain, alleviates nausea and morning sickness, and also helps those who suffer from multiple sclerosis (MS). MS is a progressive and often debilitating disease of the nervous system, caused by loss of the protective sheath that surrounds nerve fibers. The disease causes pain, muscle weakness, fatigue, and other effects that seriously diminish everyday functioning and quality of life. One of the most debilitating symptoms of the disease is muscle spasticity, a painful, involuntary contraction of muscles that hinders the ability to walk or even care for oneself. A study at the CMCR gave MS patients either marijuana or a placebo cigarette that looked and smelled like marijuana but had no active chemicals. The study concluded that marijuana provides sufferers significant relief, alleviating pain and decreasing the muscle spasms that interfere with daily life.

> "One medicine really does increase my appetite, ease the sick feeling in my stomach, help me fall asleep and calm the pain and twitching, but it's illegal: marijuana."[11]
>
> —a patient with multiple sclerosis.

One MS sufferer, who was diagnosed with the disease at age thirty-one, relates that "at 33, I have had to relearn how to walk three times. My disease has progressed rapidly, and the pain—ranging from pins and needles to shooting pains throughout my body—never goes away. . . . One medicine really does increase my appetite, ease the sick feeling in my stomach, help me fall asleep and calm the pain and twitching, but it's illegal: marijuana."[11]

A Host of Other Uses

Marijuana's effectiveness at pain management, nausea control and appetite enhancement, and alleviating muscular spasms should alone prove its medical value. But the list continues. Ongoing studies have found that marijuana can alleviate the symptoms of ADHD, stress, autism, and depression, and it has even been effective in shrinking some tumors. If any other natural substance had been found to have as many medicinal uses as marijuana, it would have been available almost immediately. What keeps marijuana out of the hands of medical patients is pure, nonsensical prejudice. The federal government should not be allowed to impede marijuana from getting to the people who need it most.

Medical Marijuana Is Not Effective Medicine

"To date, the FDA has not found smoked marijuana to be either safe or effective medicine for any condition."

Office of National Drug Control Policy, "Marijuana," November 2010. www.whitehouse.gov.

Consider these questions as you read:

1. The author says that most of the information about marijuana's therapeutic effects is anecdotal. Why does that make it difficult to assess its effectiveness?
2. What makes marijuana particularly hard to give patients as a medicine? In what ways might these obstacles be overcome?
3. Although marijuana may aid people with glaucoma, some critics argue that it may be impractical. Do you think the author's objections to its use seem credible? Why or why not?

Editor's note: The discussion that follows presents common arguments made in support of this perspective, reinforced by facts, quotes, and examples taken from various sources.

There is no reliable scientific evidence that marijuana is an effective medicine. Rigorous studies establishing its efficacy and safety are scant, and much of the purported evidence is anecdotal only. A review of evidence by the American Medical Association found fewer than twenty legitimate clinical trials on medical marijuana to date. These studies involved very few subjects—roughly three hundred. This limited scientific evidence falls far short of the evidence that is usually required for a drug to be sold in the United States.

Many people criticize the FDA for marijuana's lack of approval. The FDA is the federal agency established to regulate the release of new foods and health-related products. With a lack of rigorous studies, however, medical marijuana cannot even be submitted to the FDA for approval. There is no justification for treating marijuana differently from any other legal drug in the United States. Legal drugs such as acetaminophen, codeine, and morphine have become available only after they met the high standards established by the FDA. Unlike these drugs, marijuana has not been recommended by prestigious medical organizations such as the American Medical Association, the American Academy of Pediatrics, and the Institute of Medicine (IOM).

Dosage Varies Wildly

For marijuana to be marketed as a drug, it must have a standardized formulation and dose, have been tested in rigorous trials, and be administered via a standardized delivery system. Because marijuana is usually smoked, it is extremely difficult to establish standardized dosing. In addition, each plant varies in amounts of active components. Some strains have pronounced effects, other strains are much milder. Products made from these different strains of marijuana can vary wildly in their cannabinoid composition.

Supporters of medical marijuana often cite a 1999 IOM report because it stated that marijuana does appear to mitigate pain, appetite loss, nausea, and anxiety, arguing that the study is the equivalent of an endorsement. However, while acknowledging marijuana's benefits, the study ultimately rejects the idea of marijuana being used as a medicine. The report states that there is "little future in smoked cannabis as a medically approved medication." It concluded, moreover, that "if there is any future of marijuana as a medicine, it lies in its isolated components, the cannabinoids and their synthetic derivatives."[12]

The National Institute on Drug Abuse (NIDA), an agency of the National Institutes of Health, conducts research related to drug abuse and uses this information to guide public policy. According to Robert DuPont, the former director of NIDA, "Never in the history of modern medicine has burning leaves been considered medicine. Those of the medical marijuana movement are putting on white coats and expressing concerns about the sick. But people need to see this for what it is . . . a fraud and a hoax."[13]

No Medical Value

All drugs that are considered a controlled substance under federal law are divided into one of five schedules. To date, the federal government has classified marijuana as a Schedule 1 drug with no medical value.

Schedule I Controlled Substances

Substances in this schedule have no currently accepted medical use in the United States, a lack of accepted safety for use under medical supervision, and a high potential for abuse.

Some examples of substances listed in Schedule I are heroin, LSD, marijuana, and ecstasy.

Schedule II Controlled Substances

Substances in this schedule have a high potential for abuse which may lead to severe psychological or physical dependence.

Examples of Schedule II substances include oxycodone, morphine, opium, and codeine.

Schedule III Controlled Substances

Substances in this schedule have a potential for abuse less than substances in Schedules I or II and abuse may lead to moderate or low physical dependence or high psychological dependence.

Examples of Schedule III substances include Vicodin, Tylenol with codeine, Ketamine, and anabolic steroids.

Schedule IV Controlled Substances

Substances in this schedule have a low potential for abuse relative to substances in Schedule III.

Examples of Schedule IV substances include Xanax and Soma.

Schedule V Controlled Substances

Substances in this schedule have a low potential for abuse relative to substances listed in Schedule IV and consist primarily of preparations containing limited quantities of certain narcotics.

Examples of Schedule V substances include certain cough medicines containing codeine.

Source: Office of Diversion Control, US Department of Justice, Drug Enforcement Administration, September 2012.
www.deadiversion.usdoj.gov.

Glaucoma

Whether smoked or taken in other forms, such as a pill, a variety of studies show that marijuana is not effective for many of the diseases and disorders it is purported to treat. Even if it did treat some diseases, marijuana is unnecessary because far more effective medicines already exist that have undergone rigorous testing. The medical treatment of glaucoma is a prime example.

Glaucoma is a serious eye disorder marked by an increase in intraocular pressure that, if left untreated, can lead to blindness. In fact, glaucoma is the leading cause of blindness in the United States. The few studies that have researched marijuana as an effective glaucoma treatment, however, had less than miraculous results. The National Eye Institute concluded that none of these studies proved that "marijuana—or any of its components—could lower IOP [intraocular pressure] as effectively as drugs already on the market. In addition, some potentially serious side effects were noted, including an increased heart rate and a decrease in blood pressure in studies using smoked marijuana."[14] The Glaucoma Research Foundation agrees that marijuana could not treat intraocular pressure "better than the variety of drugs currently on the market."[15]

> "Never in the history of modern medicine has burning leaves been considered medicine. Those of the medical marijuana movement are putting on white coats and expressing concerns about the sick. But people need to see this for what it is . . . a fraud and a hoax."[13]
>
> —Robert DuPont, the former director of NIDA.

Marijuana's side effects also prevent its widespread use. The drug impairs judgment and has other mind-altering effects that are not useful for treating the disease. It is inconceivable to think that patients who have severe, debilitating illnesses should go around stoned out of their minds all day to treat their illnesses. Likewise, when compared with newer glaucoma medications, marijuana's short-lived effect is disappointing. According to the American Academy of Pediatrics, marijuana:

only lowers IOP for a short period of time—about three or four hours. This short period of time is a major drawback for the use of marijuana as a glaucoma treatment. Because glaucoma needs to be treated 24 hours a day, you would need to smoke marijuana six to eight times a day around the clock to receive the benefit of a consistently lowered IOP. Because of marijuana's mood altering effect, smoking so much of it daily would leave you too impaired to drive, operate equipment or function at the peak of your mental ability.[16]

Multiple Sclerosis

Other diseases have similarly poor results when marijuana is used as a treatment. A May 2002 study published in the journal *Neurology* studied sixteen patients with MS with severe spasticity to assess the effect of oral THC—the most active component in marijuana—and a plant extract of the *Cannabis sativa* plant. Although both medications proved safe, Joep Killestein, a multiple sclerosis researcher at VU Medical Centre in Amsterdam and the lead author of the study, concluded that "compared to placebo, neither THC nor plant-extract treatment reduced spasticity."[17]

In 2011 Anthony Feinstein and his colleagues at the University of Toronto reviewed the data pertaining to marijuana use by MS patients. Feinstein, a professor of psychiatry, concluded that "cannabis users performed significantly more poorly than nonusers on measures of information processing speed, working memory, executive functions, and visuospatial perception. They were also twice as likely as nonusers to be classified as globally impaired."[18]

Pain

Perhaps the most persistent and enduring myth about marijuana is that it is superior in the treatment of pain. Recent brain and nervous system research seems to contradict the claims about marijuana's effectiveness in pain relief. A recent paper published in the journal *Science* found that the endocannabinoids that are produced in the human body and are biochemically similar to cannabinoids in marijuana can actually overactivate the body's pain system, which can increase and prolong pain. According to Volker Neugebauer, a researcher at the University of Texas Medical Branch that studied these effects, "In the spinal cord there's a balance of systems that control what information, including information about pain, is transmitted to the brain. . . . Excitatory systems act like a car's accelerator, and inhibitory ones act like the brakes. What we found is that in the spinal cord endocannabinoids can disable the brakes [that dampen pain]." Neugebauer concludes: "To sum up, we've discovered a novel mechanism that can transform transient normal pain into persistent chronic pain."[19] These findings prove that marijuana is far too unproven to release to the general, unsuspecting public.

Depression

Proponents claim that marijuana is an antidepressant, but several studies indicate the opposite. While marijuana may relieve symptoms of depression and anxiety in the short term, when the effect wears off, depressed users have even higher levels of depression. Gregory Simon, a researcher at the Center for Health Studies at the Group Health Cooperative, states another reason marijuana is not an effective treatment for depression: it decreases the energy and motivation that are crucial for recovery.

> Using marijuana can certainly contribute to or worsen depression. Low motivation, fatigue, and withdrawal from positive activities are central features of depression and marijuana can worsen each of those problems. Some people do say that marijuana dulls anxiety or negative feelings. But it also dulls energy and motivation. And we know that activation and engagement are key parts of recovery from depression.[20]

Another commonly reported side effect of marijuana use is acute anxiety and panic. These symptoms would clearly undermine its use for depressed or other mentally ill patients. Although no studies have definitively linked marijuana to anxiety disorders, anecdotal reports continue to accumulate. One user describes his reaction to marijuana in this way: "I first experienced panic when I was 17 after having marijuana. It was so extreme the word panic doesn't seem strong enough. It was more like absolute terror."[21] Reports like these, though few, would clearly impact marijuana's therapeutic benefits. People who are seriously ill would have their symptoms magnified by such a fear response.

> "Low motivation, fatigue, and withdrawal from positive activities are central features of depression and marijuana can worsen each of those problems."[20]
>
> —Gregory Simon, a researcher at the Center for Health Studies at the Group Health Cooperative.

While the pro-marijuana lobby continues to work for the legalization of marijuana as a safe and harmless alternative to current drugs, research does not support such assertions. Indeed, there is enough evidence to prove that marijuana lacks the long-term studies to allow its use. Without such factual and unbiased studies, marijuana should not be approved as a medicine.

Chapter Two

Is Medical Marijuana Safe?

Medical Marijuana Is Safe

- Unlike many commonly used drugs, marijuana has a proven safety record.
- Study after study disproves perceived harmful effects of marijuana.
- Marijuana's side effects are short lived and medically insignificant.

The Debate at a Glance

Medical Marijuana Is Not Safe

- Because marijuana has not undergone rigorous FDA testing, no one knows whether it is safe.
- Marijuana may cause some cancers.
- Marijuana may cause mental disorders.

Medical Marijuana Is Safe

"When it comes to the chances of immediate death by chemical toxicity, marijuana is about a hundred times safer than alcohol."

Robert Gable, "Not All Drugs Are Created Equal," *New York Times*, December 19, 2011. www.nytimes.com.

Consider these questions as you read:

1. What tests has marijuana been subjected to that prove that it is safe? Why do people still have doubts about marijuana, in spite of the tests?
2. The author thinks that marijuana's side effects are minor. What evidence does he present to prove that this is true?
3. One of the author's main arguments in favor of medical marijuana is that other medicines are worse. Do you think this is an effective argument? Why or why not?

Editor's note: The discussion that follows presents common arguments made in support of this perspective, reinforced by facts, quotes, and examples taken from various sources.

Medical marijuana has an excellent safety record—no one has ever died from a marijuana overdose. Many scientists have concluded that the safety concerns, while real, are minor when compared with other legal drugs such as alcohol, valium, and many others. The Marijuana Policy Project, a marijuana advocacy group, puts it succinctly when it argues that "doctors are allowed to prescribe cocaine, morphine, and methamphetamine. Can anyone say with a straight face that marijuana is more dangerous than these substances?" The organization goes on to say that

> all medicines have some negative side effects. For example, Tylenol (acetaminophen) has been estimated to kill nearly 500 Americans per year by causing acute liver failure, while no one has ever died

from marijuana poisoning. But no one would seriously suggest banning Tylenol because it's too dangerous. In contrast, recent medical marijuana studies have found no significant side effects.[22]

Clearly, discounting marijuana's medical effectiveness on safety grounds is unfounded.

Toxicity

Marijuana's safety record is especially impressive when one looks at its level of toxicity in comparison with other legal drugs. The dose of marijuana necessary to produce death is exponentially higher than the dose a user would be able to consume in a day. In rodent studies, the dose of THC required to produce a 50 percent mortality rate is far higher than drugs such as codeine or Tylenol. In fact, it would be virtually impossible to fatally overdose on marijuana. Health education teacher Ron Marczyk explains:

> Acetaminophen causes three times as many cases of liver failure as all other drugs combined, and is the most common cause of acute liver failure in the United States—accounting for 39% of all cases. While it occurs through overdosing, even recommended doses, especially combined with even small amounts of alcohol, have caused irreversible liver failure. Four grams of Tylenol—that is, just eight extra-strength tabs, taken all at once—kills you by killing your liver. Have you ever heard of any person committing suicide with a marijuana overdose? No, because it is impossible. If you smoke too much you just fall asleep; that's all.[23]

Marijuana's safety was the focus of a ten-year study published in 2011. The study, conducted by Claremont Graduate University professor Robert Gable, compared the safety of twenty different recreational drugs. First, Gable determined the dose of the drug required to elicit the desired effect—for example, two shots of vodka to achieve intoxication. Next, Gable determined the lethal dose of each drug. Although such factors as height and weight affect a lethal dose of alcohol, people who die of alcohol poisoning usually consume the equivalent of twenty shots of vodka. Once the lethal dose of the drug was established, Gable divided the lethal dose by the effective dose to find the safety margin. In the case of alcohol, the safety margin is ten, meaning that it takes roughly ten times as much alcohol to kill a user as it does to intoxicate him or her. By contrast, the safety margin of marijuana is one thousand—that is, it takes roughly one thousand times as much marijuana to kill a user as it does to make him or her high. It would be virtually impossible to smoke this much marijuana, so dying of marijuana poisoning was proved to be also impossible.

> "Doctors are allowed to prescribe cocaine, morphine, and methamphetamine. Can anyone say with a straight face that marijuana is more dangerous than these substances?"[22]
>
> —The Marijuana Policy Project, a marijuana advocacy group.

No Sign of Adverse Effects

Since the primary delivery system for using marijuana is a cigarette, many scientists have surmised that smoking marijuana could lead to lung cancer. Yet the largest, longest, and most recent study to date has found little relationship between lung cancer and marijuana smoking. A twenty-year study published in January 2012 in the *Journal of the American Medical Association* concluded that marijuana does not impair lung function. Mark Pletcher, the lead author of the study, asserts that "marijuana may have beneficial effects on pain control, appetite, mood, and management of other chronic symptoms. Our findings suggest that occasional use of marijuana for these or other purposes may not be associated with adverse consequences on pulmonary function."[24]

A 2012 study conducted by Stefan Kertesz of the University of Alabama at Birmingham found no evidence of long-term loss of lung function. In fact, regular marijuana use actually seemed to improve lung function. "At levels of marijuana exposure commonly seen in Americans, occasional marijuana use was associated with increases in lung air-flow rates and increases in lung capacity," according to Kertesz. He concludes that "the data showed that even up to moderately high-use levels—one

Marijuana's Excellent Safety Record

The Centers for Disease Control and Prevention (CDC) collects information on causes of all deaths in the United States each year. The CDC's 2011 report (on deaths in 2009) shows thousands died from legal and illicit drugs, alcohol, firearms, and various health conditions, but not one death resulted from marijuana.

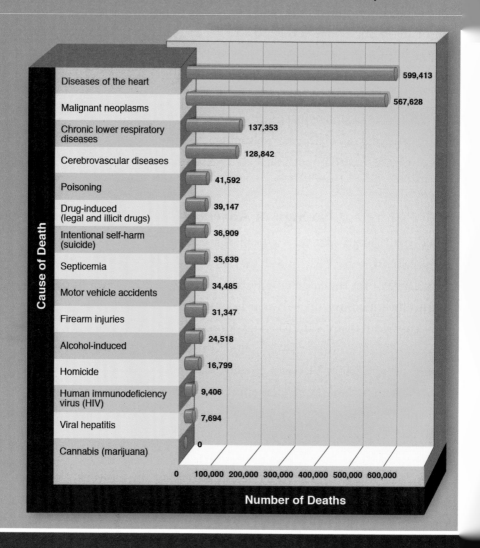

Cause of Death	Number of Deaths
Diseases of the heart	599,413
Malignant neoplasms	567,628
Chronic lower respiratory diseases	137,353
Cerebrovascular diseases	128,842
Poisoning	41,592
Drug-induced (legal and illicit drugs)	39,147
Intentional self-harm (suicide)	36,909
Septicemia	35,639
Motor vehicle accidents	34,485
Firearm injuries	31,347
Alcohol-induced	24,518
Homicide	16,799
Human immunodeficiency virus (HIV)	9,406
Viral hepatitis	7,694
Cannabis (marijuana)	0

Source: Kenneth D. Kochanek et al., "Deaths: Final Data for 2009," Division of Vital Statistics, Centers for Disease Control and Prevention. December 29, 2011. www.cdc.gov.

joint a day for seven years—there is no evidence of decreased air-flow rates or lung volumes."[25]

Even these positive findings may be a moot point. Today many marijuana users employ a vaporizer as a delivery method, so they are not even exposed to the harmful effects of smoking the drug. During vaporization, marijuana is heated and the medically active cannabinoids are released in vapor form, without smoke and its harmful by-products. A 2007 study found that vaporization produces blood levels of THC similar to those produced when marijuana is smoked, but without any adverse effects on the lungs.

One of the other supposedly harmful effects of marijuana is that it reduces immune function. A number of studies during the 1970s reported that marijuana negatively impacted the human immune system, the interconnected system of structures and cells of the human body that help fight infection and disease. Yet many scientists have criticized these studies. As AIDS specialist Mary Romeyn explains in her book *Nutrition and HIV*, these studies "used amounts far in excess of what recreational smokers, or wasting patients with prescribed medication, would actually use. . . . Looking at marijuana medically . . . this is a good drug for people with HIV."[26] Physicians who prescribe medical marijuana still find that the drug is the best treatment for pain, nausea, and appetite loss.

More recently, research on HIV patients who used medical marijuana did not show any additional damage to their already weakened immune systems. Three University of California studies published since 2007 recommended that such patients use the drug to alleviate their symptoms because the drug had little or no side effects.

Cognitive Impairment and Mood Disorders

For most users, the effects of marijuana tend to be positive. Most people report feelings of relaxation and well-being as well as enhanced sensory perceptions, for example, while listening to music and enjoying food. These results are especially helpful to those who are suffering from debilitating diseases. Marijuana does have some fairly common side effects, however, such as some minor loss of short-term memory, attention, and reaction time. Yet these effects are mild and, at the most, last only one to two hours after using marijuana. Memory returns fully after the drug leaves the system. Although some residual impairment has been noted in chronic marijuana users up to twelve weeks after quitting, a 2011 study at the Centre for Mental Health Research at Australian National University found no lingering, permanent effect on cognition. Robert Tait, the author of the study, concludes that "the adverse impacts of cannabis use on cognitive functions either appear to be related to pre-existing factors or are reversible . . . even after potentially extended periods of use."[27] Many claim, moreover, that the temporary effects of marijuana intoxication are to be expected with any mind-altering substance—such as morphine, alcohol, and many other legal substances—and should therefore not negate marijuana as effective medicine.

> "Marijuana may have beneficial effects on pain control, appetite, mood, and management of other chronic symptoms. Our findings suggest that occasional use of marijuana for these or other purposes may not be associated with adverse consequences on pulmonary function."[24]
>
> —Mark Pletcher, a researcher at the University of California at San Francisco.

The most damning marijuana evidence from critics also turns out to be fairly minor. Some people have reported feelings of intense anxiety, even psychosis, after using the drug. The risk is negligible, however, and no convincing evidence exists that marijuana causes psychosis or mental health problems in healthy individuals. Rather, a small risk of psychosis presents only in predisposed, vulnerable individuals. Countries with high rates of marijuana use do not have any higher rates of mental illnesses than other countries, for example. A 2009 study at Keele University in England examined schizophrenia rates following a substantial rise in marijuana use in the country during the 1970s. Researchers measured how many cases of schizophrenia were diagnosed between 1996 and 2005, concluding that no evidence could be found of increased schizophrenia or other forms of psychosis in the general population.

In short, clear and abundant evidence exists that medical marijuana aids people who have certain diseases. Likewise, its side effects are far less pronounced and it is far less harmful than other drugs used to treat the same symptoms. Clearly, marijuana must remain in America's drug arsenal.

Medical Marijuana Is Not Safe

"Marijuana use increases the risk of developing mental disorders by 40 percent. The risk of psychosis increases with frequency of marijuana use, from 50 to 200 percent among frequent users."

Marijuana Resource Center, Office of National Drug Control Policy, Executive Office of the President. www.whitehouse.gov.

Consider these questions as you read:

1. The author claims that marijuana is the only drug that has been approved through public opinion instead of rigorous testing. How might a reader find out whether this is accurate?
2. Much of the author's evidence of marijuana's harm is recent. Why is this significant to an understanding of marijuana's medicinal value?
3. What is marijuana's effect on IQ? Does this affect your attitude toward marijuana smoking? If so, how?

Editor's note: The discussion that follows presents common arguments made in support of this perspective, reinforced by facts, quotes, and examples taken from various sources.

There is no incontrovertible evidence that marijuana is safe. Therefore, there is no justification for treating it differently than any other drug that must be approved by the FDA. The rigorous, scientific FDA approval process remains the only legally recognized procedure for ensuring that the drugs used by Americans are safe. The FDA and many major medical associations—including the American Cancer Society, the National Multiple Sclerosis Society, and the American Glaucoma Foundation—have not found marijuana to be safe or effective. In most of the states that have legalized medical marijuana, this action has taken place through a public vote rather than through a science-based approval process. Public opinion is not a reliable measure of whether a drug should be approved as safe. No other drug has been legalized in the United States through public opinion.

According to the national agency that oversees many of America's drug policies, the Office of National Drug Control Policy (ONDCP), "Marijuana contains chemicals that can change how the brain works. And the science, while still evolving in terms of long-term consequences of marijuana use, is clear: marijuana use is associated with addiction, respiratory and mental illness, poor motor performance, and cognitive impairment, among other negative effects."[28] Moreover, the agency explicitly states that the potency of these harmful chemicals in marijuana is higher than it has ever been. According to the ONDCP, growers are breeding marijuana plants today that contain far more THC—the psychoactive compound in marijuana—than they did ten or twenty years ago. Average THC content is at an all-time high of 11 percent; some varieties have as much as 30 percent. This extremely high psychoactive content makes marijuana use an even greater concern for the public.

> "The science, while still evolving in terms of long-term consequences of marijuana use, is clear: marijuana use is associated with addiction, respiratory and mental illness, poor motor performance, and cognitive impairment, among other negative effects."[28]
>
> —The Office of National Drug Control Policy.

Lung Cancer and Other Respiratory Effects

Like tobacco smoke, marijuana smoke contains many carcinogenic ingredients that can lead to cancer and other diseases of the lungs, such as emphysema. Studies have reported that marijuana delivers four times the amount of tar, the carcinogen benzopyrene, and other dangerous substances. Marijuana also contains toxins and particles that can inflame the lining of the lungs. This could lead to bronchitis, pneumonia, and other lung disorders. This is especially dangerous to cancer or HIV-infected patients with weakened immune systems.

In addition to marijuana's effects on the lungs, other recent studies have linked it to several other cancers. A new study from the University of Southern California (USC) linked marijuana to the development of a virulent strain of testicular cancer. The study found that men with a history of marijuana use were twice as likely to have the especially virulent strains of the cancer. "We speculate that [marijuana] may be acting through the endocannabinoid system . . . since this system has been shown to be important in the formation of sperm,"[29] explains Victoria Cortessis, an assistant professor of preventive medicine at USC.

Marijuana has also been linked to DNA damage that causes cancer. Scientists at Sweden's Cancer Biomarkers and Prevention Group have reported that smoked marijuana might damage DNA: "These results provide evidence for the DNA damaging potential of cannabis smoke, implying that the consumption of cannabis cigarettes may be detrimental to human health with the possibility to initiate cancer development."[30] This ongoing study is just one of many to identify marijuana as a possible cause of serious disease.

Cardiovascular and Reproductive Issues

Some forms of heart disease, for instance, have been linked to marijuana use. Marijuana affects heart rate and blood pressure. According to NIDA, marijuana use increases heart rate by 20 to 100 percent almost immediately after inhalation. The increase in heart rate can last a full three hours. A 2008 study found that marijuana may also increase the body's production of a protein that raises levels of blood fats that have been implicated in heart attacks and strokes. According to Christopher Granger, a professor of medicine at Duke University, the study seems to confirm that marijuana "may have a real impact on the way people who use marijuana metabolize food, showing that it could have an adverse effect on cholesterol."[31] Scientists involved in the study think that the increased levels of fats found in the blood of marijuana users might actually be what causes the cardiovascular changes in heart rate and blood pressure. These results alone should make marijuana proponents adjust their thinking on its safety.

Marijuana's harmful effects also extend to the reproductive system. The drug may alter the reproductive system, so it should not be used during pregnancy. According to a report published in the *Journal of the American Academy of Child & Adolescent Psychiatry*, use of marijuana during pregnancy restricted fetal growth during mid to late pregnancy and resulted in lower-birth-weight babies. The report concluded that "maternal cannabis use, even for a short period, may be associated with several adverse fetal growth trajectories."[32]

Mental Health Concerns

People have long used marijuana to alter their mental state, so it should be no surprise to find that recent studies have implicated it in increasing mental health diseases. Using marijuana, even for the purpose of alleviating pain or nausea, may predispose patients to a variety of psychological problems, such as short-term memory loss, stupor, lowered IQ, anxiety, and psychotic experiences, including schizophrenia.

One commonly reported side effect is acute anxiety and panic. "The room was spinning," one marijuana user says of his reaction to the drug. "There was buzzing in my ears, my heart was thumping, I was sweating all over. Felt like I could hardly breathe, that I was going to die."[33] These adverse responses would eliminate marijuana's positive effects in some seriously ill people.

The link between marijuana and other mental disorders is especially troubling. For example, marijuana use has been linked to the onset of schizophrenia and other forms of psychosis. One significant 2011 study at the University of Amsterdam found an association between marijuana use and the onset of psychosis, especially in young marijuana users. D.H. Linszen, a professor of psychiatry and the lead researcher, asserts that the "younger age at onset of cannabis use or a cannabis use disorder was significantly related to younger age at onset of six symptoms. Onset of cannabis use preceded symptoms in most participants." Linszen concludes that the study's "results provide support that cannabis use plays an important role in the development of psychosis in vulnerable individuals. Cannabis use in early adolescence should be discouraged."[34]

Other studies seem to confirm such conclusions. Joseph M. Pierre, the chief physician at the Schizophrenia Treatment Unit at the Veterans Administration West Los Angeles Healthcare Center, wrote in a 2011 article that several studies done in the past fifteen years "provide strong support for an association between cannabis use as an adolescent or young adult and a greater risk for developing a psychotic disorder such as schizophrenia." Although Pierre concedes that "a causal relationship has not been firmly established," he concludes that "current evidence supports that cannabis is a 'component' cause of chronic psychosis."[35]

Other studies point to the harms of long-term marijuana use, particularly in those who started using marijuana as teenagers. A 2012 study of adults

Marijuana Is Dangerous

The use of marijuana, even for medical purposes, poses grave risks. Hundreds of thousands of patients sought emergency room treatment for problems associated with marijuana use in 2010, more than double those seeking treatment for health problems related to heroin use.

Misused or Abused Drug Most Commonly Involved in Emergency Department Visits: 2010

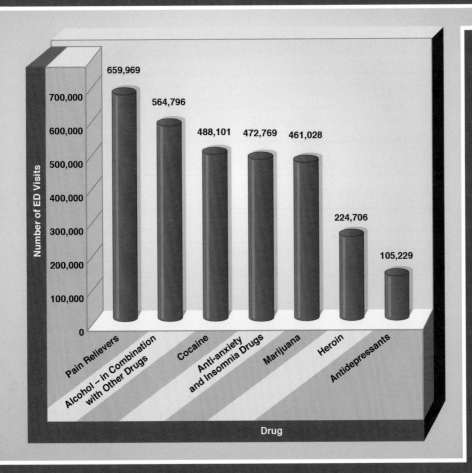

Source: SAMHSA Drug Abuse Warning Network, *The Dawn Report: Highlights of the 2010 Drug Abuse Warning Network (DAWN) Findings on Drug-Related Emergency Department Visits*, July 2, 2012. www.samhsa.gov.

who started using marijuana regularly before the age of eighteen showed an average decline in IQ of eight points. The results of the study of more than one thousand New Zealanders were released in August 2012. Madeline Meier, a postdoctoral researcher at Duke University, claims that "marijuana is not harmless, particularly for adolescents." The decline in IQ among long-term marijuana users could not be explained by alcohol, other drug use, or educational level. "Somebody who loses 8 IQ points as an adolescent may be disadvantaged compared to their same-age peers for years to come,"[36] Meier concludes. These results are significant, especially when some doctors are advocating the use of marijuana to treat autism, attention deficit disorder, and depression in teens.

> "Cannabis use plays an important role in the development of psychosis in vulnerable individuals. Cannabis use in early adolescence should be discouraged."[34]
>
> —D.H. Linszen, a professor of psychiatry.

A Bad Idea

Marijuana's dark side is slowly being revealed as it is studied more fully. Most of the reported safety of medical marijuana is purely anecdotal, based on collective personal experience and not on rigorous scientific tests. According to NIDA, these studies and many others should preclude marijuana's use:

> Marijuana is not an FDA approved medicine. . . . There are several reasons why marijuana is an unlikely medication candidate: (1) it is an unpurified plant containing numerous chemicals with unknown health effects, (2) it is typically consumed by smoking, further contributing to potential adverse effects, and its non-patentable status makes it an unattractive investment for pharmaceutical companies. The promise lies instead in medications developed from marijuana's active components, the cannabinoids, or (perhaps less so) for the development of alternative delivery systems for marijuana consumption.[37]

If marijuana does have potential medical use, it should, as NIDA suggests, be developed in the laboratory, not from a plant that varies in its effects.

Chapter Three

Should Medical Marijuana Be Legalized?

Medical Marijuana Should Not Be Legalized

- Marijuana is addictive.
- Marijuana leads to hard-core drug use.
- Legalized marijuana increases crime and violence.

The Debate at a Glance

Medical Marijuana Should Be Legalized

- Marijuana is not addictive.
- Legalized medical marijuana does not increase marijuana use among teens.
- Legalizing medical marijuana may decrease crime.

Medical Marijuana Should Not Be Legalized

"Several studies have shown that marijuana dependence is real and causes harm. . . . The lifetime prevalence of marijuana dependence in the US population is higher than that for any other illicit drug."

R. Gil Kerlikowske, "Why Marijuana Legalization Would Compromise Public Health and Public Safety," statement delivered at the California Police Chiefs Association Conference, March 4, 2010. www.white house.gov.

Consider these questions as you read:

1. The author uses a statistic and a piece of anecdotal evidence to make the claim that marijuana leads to hard-core drug abuse. Which do you find more convincing? Why?
2. Why do most people use marijuana, according to the author? Do you agree? Why or why not?
3. The author quotes members of law enforcement to prove that marijuana use increases crime. Might such sources be biased? Why or why not?

Editor's note: The discussion that follows presents common arguments made in support of this perspective, reinforced by facts, quotes, and examples taken from various sources.

There are a multitude of reasons why medical marijuana should remain illegal. One of the most obvious is that people who start using marijuana will inevitably turn to other, more addictive drugs. This is why marijuana is frequently called a gateway drug. This is not personal opinion; hard-core drug addicts often say that they started with marijuana. According to NIDA, pot users are 104 times more likely to use cocaine than are those who have never tried pot. The US government has consistently noted this as one reason for its hard line on marijuana.

An Addictive Drug

Despite its reputation as a relatively harmless drug, marijuana is addictive. Although it is not as powerfully addictive on first use as more hard-core drugs such as heroin, many users do become addicted. As clinical psychologist Lynn O'Connor describes in *Psychology Today*, "Marijuana addiction is absolutely pernicious; it's subtle, deceptive, and often hidden, even to the user, while its effects pervade every corner of the user's life. . . . Pot use is a sure way to put yourself in a chemical jacket." According to O'Connor, marijuana addiction presents itself as a lack of ambition, or caring, about one's life. "Ambitious people lower or even drop their ambitions."[38] Many people casually use marijuana to treat a multitude of problems, arguing that it is safer than conventional treatments. It is only once they begin to use the drug that they are marked by its addictive qualities, which can lead to the same problems as other addictive substances.

Writer Cassie Rodenberg found herself addicted to marijuana when she could not stop using it. "I was dumping out trash cans with ashes at the bottom so I could pick through and make a pile of charred green that I could smoke. For the next two years my life fluctuated between weeks of being high and weeks of being clean, trying to make up for late homework and ignored relationships." Because of widespread misinformation that marijuana was not addictive, Rodenberg doubted herself, thinking that it was not the pot that was making her do the things she was doing but rather her own psychological issues. As she describes, "I had no idea of the destructive potential of weed. . . . The lack of info about the addictive potential of marijuana only feeds the vacuum of ignorance that sucks people deeper and deeper into addiction."[39]

> "Marijuana addiction is absolutely pernicious; it's subtle, deceptive, and often hidden, even to the user, while its effects pervade every corner of the user's life. . . . Pot use is a sure way to put yourself in a chemical jacket."[38]
>
> —Lynn O'Connor, a clinical psychologist.

Legalization Equals More Drug Users

Clearly, marijuana is not a harmless drug. Yet those who want to make a profit from the drug hope that legalizing medical marijuana will lead to

Poor Candidate for Legalization

Statistics show high levels of abuse and dependence among marijuana users. Legalizing medical marijuana is likely to raise those levels. According to the National Survey on Drug Use and Health, which tracks drug usage trends in the United States, marijuana was the illicit drug most commonly associated with drug dependence or abuse by users aged twelve or older who used the drug in the year before the survey.

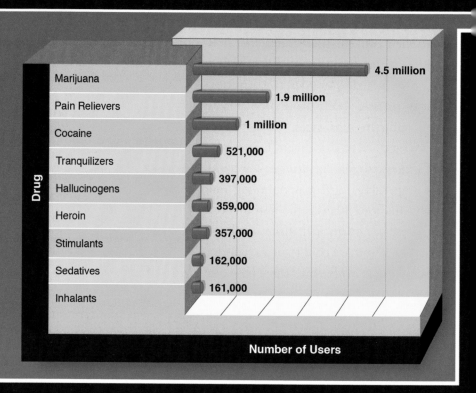

Specific Illicit Drug Dependence or Abuse in the Past Year Among Persons Aged Twelve or Older: 2010

Drug	Number of Users
Marijuana	4.5 million
Pain Relievers	1.9 million
Cocaine	1 million
Tranquilizers	521,000
Hallucinogens	397,000
Heroin	359,000
Stimulants	357,000
Sedatives	162,000
Inhalants	161,000

Source: SAMHSA, National Survey on Drug Use and Health, 2010. www.samhsa.gov.

legalizing all marijuana. These profiteers hope to increase the drug's use and benefit from its popularity, especially among young people. Legalizing medical marijuana promotes the message that marijuana is harmless, which will lead to wider usage and wider availability. Melinda Haag, US attorney for California's northern district, has shut down dispensaries that operate in areas that could impact children and teens. She says: "I receive letters from people who tell me things like my business is across the street from a high school and a dispensary and I watch kids all day long go in and out and then into the high school. And then I hear that they have a tremendous problem in that high school with marijuana use by students."[40]

Legalizing medical marijuana makes it easier for adolescents to obtain it. If one teen has a prescription, he or she can share it with peers. In fact, a study published in the July 2012 issue of the *Journal of the American Academy of Child & Adolescent Psychiatry* found that this is very common. After interviewing teens in substance abuse programs in the Denver area, 73.8 percent said that they had obtained marijuana from someone with a prescription. Once medical marijuana is legalized, it would be nearly impossible to keep it out of the hands of vulnerable teens.

Already, there is strong evidence that people are using medical marijuana to get high as opposed to treating medical disorders. Proponents say that it is necessary for the treatment of cancer, HIV, multiple sclerosis, and glaucoma. A 2011 study in the *Journal of Drug Policy Analysis*, however, examined 1,655 applicants in California seeking a doctor's recommendation for medical marijuana use. The study found that less than 5 percent requested prescriptions to ease the symptoms from these diseases.

In California, where medical marijuana is legal, the state is seeing just such an increase in use. California voters had no intention of allowing widespread use of marijuana when they passed the medical marijuana law in 1996, yet that is exactly what is happening. According to an Associated Press editorial, "California voters rejected a proposed law in 2010 that would have legalized marijuana. What growers and dealers there are doing now is trying to use the medical marijuana system to accomplish what they failed to do at the ballot box."[41]

According to the Colorado Department of Health, less than 1 percent of medical marijuana users in Colorado used pot to alleviate symptoms of HIV, and only 2 percent used it for cancer. Overwhelmingly, 94 percent used if for "severe pain"—a vague description that could be something or nothing. This data makes it clear that most people are not using medical marijuana for untreatable or life-threatening medical conditions. Instead, unscrupulous doctors are writing prescriptions in exchange for a fee.

Drugs Increase Crime

Where drugs go, so does an increase in crime, and marijuana is no exception. In California, for example, many cities report criminal activity in areas where dispensaries are located. According to some reports, as many as six hundred medical marijuana dispensaries in California have been shut down since 2011 because of concerns about crime and violence. Haag contends: "Marijuana dispensaries are full of cash and they're full of marijuana and everybody knows that. . . . They are at risk of being robbed and many of them are robbed. . . . When a dispensary comes to my attention that is close to a school, a park, a playground or children, that's a line I've decided to draw."[42] Not only do these dispensaries create an environment that perpetuates crime and violence, but law enforcement officers are drawn away from other duties to patrol these areas.

Police officers confirm an increase in crime around medical marijuana dispensaries. Sergeant Andrew Pettit of the Sacramento Police Department relates his experience: "I have personal knowledge of crimes that have happened based around dispensaries; robberies, thefts, people either robbing businesses themselves or patrons or customers after they leave. . . . It's pretty obvious after a person goes into a dispensary and they leave, it's obvious what they have in their possession. It's like going to the bank."[43]

People who buy medical marijuana are not the only ones affected by these crimes. Residents of nearby neighborhoods must also put up with an increase in crime and violence. This reduces the value of their houses and exposes them—and their children—to unsavory elements. Some of these people might be able to sell their houses and move to better neighborhoods, but many cannot.

The Perils of Driving While Stoned

Legalizing medical marijuana would put one more drug on the street that would not only increase crime but also the likelihood of users driving under the influence. According to Jill Cooper, an associate director of the Safe Transportation Research and Education Center at the University of California at Berkeley,

> The chemicals in marijuana have been proven to interfere with key driving skills: attentiveness, visual scanning, orientation ability and basic motor skills, as well as perception of time and speed. While claims have been made that marijuana use could make people safer drivers since they tend to drive more slowly while under its influence, the alleged safety benefits are speculative, at best.[44]

A 2012 study in the *British Medical Journal* analyzed the results of twelve studies of more than forty-nine thousand people to review marijuana's effect on driving. The researchers found that those driving under the influence of marijuana were twice as likely to have a car crash as those not under the influence. Analysis by researchers at Columbia University, published in 2011, reports that stoned drivers are twice as likely as other drivers to be involved in an accident. It does not take a scientist, however, to state the obvious: driving while under the influence of any substance can and will impair the driver.

> **"The chemicals in marijuana have been proven to interfere with key driving skills: attentiveness, visual scanning, orientation ability and basic motor skills, as well as perception of time and speed."[44]**
>
> —Jill Cooper, an associate director of the Safe Transportation Research and Education Center at the University of California at Berkeley.

For many reasons, then, legalizing medical marijuana is not the humane solution for people who are in pain or suffering from disease. These people are being used as an excuse by those in the pro-marijuana lobby to increase the availability of and use of marijuana.

Medical Marijuana Should Be Legalized

"By keeping marijuana illegal, we nudge youngsters into contact with real criminals engaged in the drug trade."

Quoted in *New York Times*, "The Law Adds to the Harm," December 19, 2011. www.nytimes.com.

Consider these questions as you read:

1. One argument in favor of legalizing medical marijuana is that it is far less harmful than other legal drugs. Do you find this argument convincing? Why or why not?

2. Shutting down dispensaries where medical marijuana is legal is a catch-22: although the state allows patients to use marijuana, the law makes it difficult to obtain the drug. Can you think of other, similar situations? Do you agree or disagree with the author on this point? Why?

3. The author argues that driving while under the influence of marijuana is less dangerous than driving under the influence of alcohol and, therefore, should not be an argument against legalization. Do you agree? Why or why not?

Editor's note: The discussion that follows presents common arguments made in support of this perspective, reinforced by facts, quotes, and examples taken from various sources.

The time has come to legalize medical marijuana. The arguments against it—that users will become addicts and move on to more dangerous drugs, that crime will increase, that use among young people will rise—have no basis in fact. One of the most persistent of these arguments is that marijuana is a gateway drug, meaning that it leads users to stronger drugs. However, studies have failed to confirm this progression. In 2009, for example, 2.3 million people reported using marijuana, but only 617,000 used cocaine and 180,000 had tried heroin. While marijuana is the most-used illegal drug in the United States, it rarely leads to a worsening drug problem.

In the Netherlands and Portugal, where marijuana use is legal—and not just for medical purposes—rates of abuse of illicit drugs are no higher than in other countries. Marijuana is openly sold in Dutch coffee shops in hopes of making users less likely to resort to illegal sources that might tempt them into trying more dangerous drugs. In other words, the law was intended to separate and isolate the hard-core drug market from the marijuana market.

Common Painkillers Have Higher Risks

For those who worry about addiction, marijuana should actually be seen as a good alternative to drugs commonly used for pain and other medical conditions. In an age when more and more people are becoming addicted to prescription drugs such as OxyContin and Vicodin, marijuana seems almost harmless in comparison. Prescription opiate painkillers killed nearly fifteen thousand people in the United States in 2008. One would be hard pressed to find even one person who died from a marijuana overdose or addiction. As psychologist Jann Gumbiner argues, "It is estimated that 32 percent of tobacco users will become addicted, 23 percent of heroin users, 17 percent of cocaine users, and 15 percent of alcohol users. Cocaine and heroin are more physically harmful and nicotine is much more addictive. It is much harder

> "It is much harder to quit smoking cigarettes than it is to quit smoking pot."[45]
>
> —psychologist Jann Gumbiner.

to quit smoking cigarettes than it is to quit smoking pot."[45] People who are ill and in pain need to at least have the option of using medical marijuana, which offers relief without the risk of addiction or overdose.

No Link Between Medical Marijuana and Teen Use

The federal government has long maintained that legalizing medical marijuana will lead to widespread use and abuse of the drug, especially among teens. This claim is a fallacy, as several studies have proven. After

47

California passed proposition 215, for example, fears that legalized medical marijuana would send the wrong message to youth and result in increased drug use never became reality. A body of research compares states that have legalized medical marijuana to very similar states that have not. One study compared Rhode Island, which legalized medical marijuana, to Massachusetts, which did not. Esther Choo, an assistant professor of emergency medicine at Brown University and the leader of the study, used data collected from the Centers for Disease Control and Prevention from 1997 to 2009. The study involved about thirteen thousand teens in Rhode Island and twenty-five thousand teens in Massachusetts. The study concluded that in any given year, 30 percent of the teens used marijuana within the previous month. So, although marijuana use was common among teens, its legal status had little effect on teen use. Choo thinks that the population that uses medical marijuana, usually very sick adults, does not inspire its use among teens: "Whether they are taking it for pain or for vomiting control or appetite, this is not a group we think of as super inspiring for young people to take up their drug pattern."[46]

Another study published in 2012 looked at teenagers in thirteen states to see whether legalization of medical marijuana in those states led to increased use among teens. According to Daniel I. Rees, a professor of economics at the University of Colorado at Denver, and a leader of the study, "There is anecdotal evidence that medical marijuana is finding its way into the hands of teenagers, but there's no statistical evidence that legalization increases the probability of use."[47] Such studies prove, and continue to prove, that legalizing medical marijuana does not increase teen drug use.

Legalization Does Not Increase Crime

A common concern, especially among members of the law enforcement community, is that an increase in crime and violence will occur around medical marijuana dispensaries. Reasonable though this might sound, it has not come to pass in states that have legalized medical marijuana. A University of California, Los Angeles, study published in 2012 found no relation between density of dispensaries and crime. According to the report, "There were no observed cross-sectional associations between the

Growing Support for Medical Marijuana

According to a 2010 Pew Research poll, support for medical marijuana is growing. Today, nearly 73 percent of Americans report that they favor allowing the sale and use of marijuana for medical purposes.

Should your state allow the sale and use of marijuana for medical purposes?		March 2010
Favor		73%
Oppose		23%
Don't know		4%
Should the use of marijuana be made legal?	**2008**	**2010**
Yes	35%	41%
No	57%	52%
Don't know	8%	7%

Source: Pew Research Center, "Broad Public Support for Legalizing Medical Marijuana," April 1, 2010. www.pewresearch.org.

density of medical marijuana dispensaries and either violent or property crime rates."[48] A 2011 Rand Corporation study had similar results: "We found no evidence that medical marijuana dispensaries in general cause crime to rise."[49]

These unfounded fears have led to dispensary shutdowns, often leaving patients with medical marijuana prescriptions unable to obtain the needed drug. Patient Mark Maginn relates his experience:

Like hundreds of thousands of others, I turned to medical marijuana for relief from chronic pain. . . . A few months ago I went to my favorite medical marijuana dispensary in Berkeley, CA, only to find that it was told by the federal government to shut its doors because it was too close to an elementary school. . . . I have a prescription from my physician for the use of medical marijuana, as well as a state identification card that I have to show to gain entrance into a dispensary.[50]

Such closures hardly make sense. Although the state acknowledges marijuana's usefulness by allowing doctors to prescribe it, at the same time it makes it difficult for patients to obtain the drug. Once medical marijuana can be used legally in a state, governments should not be allowed to erode that right by closing dispensaries.

In fact, keeping medical marijuana illegal actually increases crime by encouraging a thriving black market. Paul Armentano, the director of the National Organization for the Reform of Marijuana Laws (NORML), asserts that "the black-market inflated price of cannabis exposes its producers and consumers to potential crime and theft from other criminal entities looking to exploit the drug's prohibition-inflated economic value. Each of these potential risks would be mitigated, if not eliminated, under a system of cannabis legalization."[51] The lesson of alcohol prohibition proves that keeping a substance illegal not only does not prevent its use but also allows traffickers to take over the market.

The Risks of Driving Stoned Are Overblown

Recently, the battle against medical marijuana has been fueled by increased fears that users will drive while under the influence. This argument seems to ignore the fact that hundreds of prescription and even over-the-counter drugs cause drowsiness or impairment, yet no one would advocate denying patients the relief they provide. Rather, we expect them to exercise personal responsibility and not drive under the influence.

Driving under the influence of any drug, even legal drugs used medically, is illegal. Many prescription drugs carry warnings not to drive, and marijuana should be similarly regulated. States already have experience enforcing drunk-driving laws. Blood alcohol tests are widely used to prevent and/or prosecute drivers who drive while under the influence. States could similarly establish a legal limit and test for blood levels of THC.

In addition, when compared with alcohol, the effects of marijuana on drivers' motor skills are far milder. In fact, one 2011 study revealed that laws legalizing medical marijuana had resulted in a 9 percent drop in traffic deaths and a 5 percent drop in beer sales among teenagers. Rees argues that his "research suggests that the legalization of medical marijuana reduces traffic fatalities through reducing alcohol consumption by young adults."[52]

Rees and coauthor D. Mark Anderson surmise that part of the decrease may be due to the fact that marijuana tends to be used in private rather than public locations. Such studies suggest that marijuana may have some clear advantages even if teens do get hold of the substance. Retired police chief Joseph D. McNamara agrees: "No one ever died from using marijuana, unlike alcohol or cocaine. Marijuana tends to mellow people, but we know alcohol and cocaine excites some into violence. Driving under any of these drugs is a no-no, but cocaine and alcohol are more likely to produce speeding and reckless driving than marijuana is."[53]

> "Research suggests that the legalization of medical marijuana reduces traffic fatalities through reducing alcohol consumption by young adults."[52]
>
> —Daniel I. Rees, a professor of economics at the University of Colorado, Denver.

Marijuana has been increasingly studied since medical marijuana laws have been passed. These studies continue to prove that there is little to no negative impact of these laws, and the lack of them increases the suffering of those with AIDS, cancer, and other diseases. It is time to end the irrational campaign against medical marijuana.

Chapter Four

Can States Adequately Regulate Medical Marijuana?

States Cannot Adequately Regulate Medical Marijuana

- States have a poor track record on regulating medical substances.
- Gaps in state laws make medical marijuana unsafe for consumers.
- States are unable to ensure that medical marijuana dispensaries serve legitimately ill people.

The Debate at a Glance

States Can Adequately Regulate Medical Marijuana

- Since states have legalized medical marijuana, federal agencies should respect state marijuana laws.
- States are improving the regulation of the sale of marijuana.
- Medically needy patients have a right to use marijuana in states that have approved it.

States Cannot Adequately Regulate Medical Marijuana

"California [medical marijuana] 'clinics' . . . have been operating as storefront drug dealers and using the humanitarian law as a screen for criminal operations."

Associated Press, "Our View: California Pot Businesses Set Bad Example for Maine," *Portland (ME) Press Herald,* October 12, 2011. www.pressherald.com.

Consider these questions as you read:

1. Do you think marijuana should remain classified as a schedule 1 substance? Explain your thinking.
2. Why does the author think that medical marijuana dispensaries deserve to be shut down? Do you agree or disagree with this point of view? Why?
3. What does the president say about the need for federal oversight of marijuana? What makes such a goal difficult to achieve?

Editor's note: The discussion that follows presents common arguments made in support of this perspective, reinforced by facts, quotes, and examples taken from various sources.

Medical marijuana is currently legal in eighteen states and the District of Columbia. Unfortunately, state governments were not prepared for the passage of such laws by public referendum. States do not know how to regulate medical marijuana's production, dispensing, and sale to ensure that it does not fall into the hands of recreational drug users and young adults. Such laws also directly contradict the federal government's need to regulate dangerous drugs. Thus, states are in an almost impossible situation when they try to regulate a substance that the federal government deems illegal. In fact, the federal government continues to view medical marijuana unfit for use as a medicine. In June 2011 the US Drug

Enforcement Administration (DEA) once again denied a petition to re-schedule marijuana. In defending the decision, DEA administrator Michele M. Leonhart argued that marijuana's "chemistry is not known and studies have not been done on its usefulness or safety. . . . At this time the known risks of marijuana use have not been shown to be outweighed by specific benefits in well-controlled clinical trials that scientifically evaluate safety and efficacy."[54]

Too Many Inadequacies

State and local laws that regulate medical marijuana are inadequate or poorly enforced and therefore fail to protect the consumer. For example, many states do not require dispensaries to inspect their suppliers or test for potency. Even if adequate state or municipal laws are in place to protect the consumer, they are often not followed and poorly enforced. Many suppliers and dispensaries are out of compliance with state laws.

Worse, many dispensaries are clearly set up as fronts to sell marijuana, not to help ill patients seeking a valid treatment. Thea Sagen, aged sixty-two, suffers from severe neuroendocrine cancer and lives in Seaside, California. When her oncologist recommended that she use marijuana to ease her pain and nausea, she entered a dispensary, expecting it to be similar to a pharmacy. Instead, Sagen found that the employees could not tell her which type of marijuana to use. Sagen recalls, "They said, 'it's trial and error.' I was in there flying blind, looking at all this stuff."[55] Sagen's experience proves that these dispensaries are nothing more than places where potheads can buy their drug of choice.

The experience of California helps reveal just how difficult it is to regulate marijuana dispensaries. In that state, prosecutors shut down hundreds of dispensaries in 2011 for not complying with the law. These lawmakers have discovered that many dispensaries are simply out to make money, not to help sick people. As Benjamin B. Wagner, US attorney for the eastern district of California claims, "We're not concerned in prosecuting patients or people who are legitimate caregivers for ill people, who are in good faith complying with state law. But we are concerned

States Cannot Adequately Regulate Medical Marijuana

The average potency of marijuana has increased sharply since 1986. At the same time, marijuana usage and admission to drug treatment centers for marijuana abuse are also on the rise. These trends lead many to believe that federal oversight is necessary to regulate marijuana for both recreational and medical use.

Marijuana Treatment Admissions and Average Potency: 1986–2010

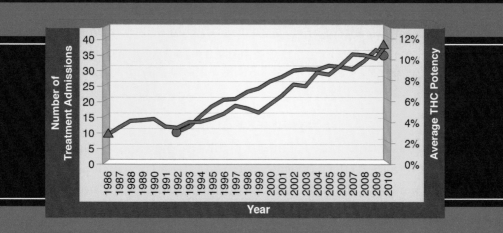

● 10,000s of primary marijuana treatment admissions
▲ Average seizure potency

Source: NSDUH, TEDS, National Seizure System/Office of National Drug Control Policy, 2010. https://nsduhweb.rti.org.

about large commercial operations that are generating huge amounts of money by selling marijuana in this essentially unregulated free-for-all that exists in California."[56]

According to US attorney Joseph Russoniello, medical marijuana dispensaries in California flout federal and state laws and become legitimate targets of federal oversight: "About 96 to 98 percent of all of the operators and all the dispensaries certainly in the state were out of compliance with the state guidelines."[57]

It is not surprising that dispensaries have a difficult time following the guidelines. California is woefully inadequate in overseeing dispensaries and at establishing a regulatory infrastructure to enforce the law. Again, California is suffering the consequences. The *Los Angeles Times* concludes that "the vagueness of state law and conflicting judicial interpretations make it well nigh impossible for anyone in California to be in clear and unambiguous compliance."[58] Making a drug legal while the federal government views it as illegal, and then attempting to make sure the drug stays in the hands of those who have prescriptions only, is proving to be a difficult task.

> "About 96 to 98 percent of all of the operators and all the dispensaries certainly in the state were out of compliance with the state guidelines."[57]
>
> —US attorney Joseph Russoniello.

Dispensaries Are Fronts

Although patients with legitimate marijuana prescriptions are clearly caught in a legal tangle between state and federal laws, such people are in the minority. The entire medical marijuana industry is a front to sell marijuana to whoever wants it. Marijuana dispensaries are distasteful, and they attract other businesses, such as tattoo parlors and porn shops, that are equally distasteful. In California, 185 cities and counties have banned pot dispensaries entirely. In New Jersey, rules on where dispensaries can locate are so restrictive that it is virtually impossible to operate a dispensary there. State medical marijuana laws are bad laws and benefit no one, especially the legitimate patients who must attempt to seek out a legitimate place to get help.

Since the first marijuana law passed in California in 1996, how marijuana should be regulated to mitigate concerns remains unsolved. Even though polls have found that the vast majority of Americans—77 percent according to a 2011 CBS News poll—approve of legalized medical marijuana, no one wants a pot shop in their neighborhood. This suggests that many Americans lack confidence that the state can adequately regulate these dispensaries and determine where they can, and should, be located.

California is not alone in having difficulty regulating marijuana. In Michigan, laws have generated confusion over who can grow and distribute marijuana and what medical uses are legitimate. With little consensus on whether marijuana helps or hinders certain medical conditions, patients who try marijuana may find it does not help them, and they have no regulatory agency to turn to when something goes wrong. As Senator Rick Jones says, "A good example is glaucoma; I've had numerous experts testify they have had patients stop their eye drops, only use marijuana and are now blind."[59]

Many of the state laws that legalize medical marijuana were enacted by public referendum. People who voted for these laws had no understanding of how they would impact society. They had no further thoughts than to help people who they believed were needlessly suffering. But laws to regulate drugs should not be passed by average people, no matter how kindhearted. Drugs must be legitimately regulated and sold in a legitimate way. What the states have now is a hodgepodge that can land even the neediest patient in jail.

> "The vagueness of state law and conflicting judicial interpretations [regarding medical marijuana] make it well nigh impossible for anyone in California to be in clear and unambiguous compliance."[58]
>
> —*Los Angeles Times* editorial.

Hindering the Nation's War on Drugs

Having states regulate medical marijuana directly conflicts with the federal government's mission to prosecute large-scale drug operations that supply recreational users. Such conflict places an unfair burden on the federal government, which must try to distinguish between legitimate medical patients and illegal recreational users.

When the federal government raids medical marijuana dispensaries, marijuana advocates accuse it of violating state laws. Yet the federal government must have free rein to keep large-scale drug operations in check. As US attorney general Eric Holder said in 2009, "Given the limited resources [of the federal government] . . . our focus will be on people, organizations that are growing, cultivating substantial amounts of marijuana and doing so in a way that's inconsistent with federal and state law."[60]

In April 2012 President Barack Obama, who, in 2008 made a campaign pledge not to use the resources of the Justice Department to override state medical marijuana laws, made it clear that federal enforcement of the nation's drug laws is crucial to society. Clarifying the position of the federal government, Obama stated that attempting to respect medical marijuana laws could not take precedence over prosecuting illegal drug traffickers and large-scale commercial operations:

> What I specifically said was that we were not going to prioritize prosecutions of persons who are using medical marijuana. I never made a commitment that somehow we were going to give carte blanche to large-scale producers and operators of marijuana—and the reason is, because it's against federal law. I can't nullify congressional law. I can't ask the Justice Department to say, "Ignore completely a federal law that's on the books." What I can say is, "Use your prosecutorial discretion and properly prioritize your resources to go after things that are really doing folks damage."
>
> [In the case of] large-scale, commercial operations that may supply medical marijuana users, but in some cases may also be supplying recreational users . . . we put the Justice Department in a very difficult place if we're telling them, "This is supposed to be against the law, but we want you to turn the other way."[61]

The Purview of the Federal Government

The states are simply not equipped to build an infrastructure to properly regulate medical marijuana. Oversight of medical marijuana must remain with the federal government.

States Can Adequately Regulate Medical Marijuana

"Generally, these laws [governing medical marijuana at the state level] are working well and providing patients with relief and protection from arrest."

Marijuana Policy Project, "Medical Marijuana Overview," 2012. www.mpp.org.

Consider these questions as you read:

1. Do you think that marijuana should remain classified as a schedule 1 substance? Why or why not?
2. Alcohol and other potentially dangerous drugs are legal or have fewer restrictions than marijuana. Do you think this makes sense? Why or why not?
3. How do marijuana laws in Colorado and Connecticut prove that marijuana can be restricted for medical use only? Do you think these laws are necessary? Explain?

Editor's note: the discussion that follows presents common arguments made in support of this perspective, reinforced by facts, quotes, and examples taken from various sources.

In many states the American public has given its approval of medical marijuana, and the federal government should not be allowed to override the laws unique to each state. As of November 2012, eighteen states and the District of Columbia have chosen to protect the right of citizens to use medical marijuana, yet the federal government continues to fight an expensive and useless war against these state laws.

Marijuana's Federal Drug Status Should Be Changed

Additionally, federal regulations stand in the way of scientific progress. To get a drug approved as a medicine requires thorough testing—and government approval for the testing. Medical marijuana's status as a schedule 1 controlled substance and federal drug control laws make these necessary clinical trials almost impossible. In order to obtain marijuana legally for research, labs must secure it from NIDA or receive federal money to support the research. If marijuana's schedule 1 status were changed, valuable clinical research into marijuana-based medicines could be conducted. Once research was complete, the process could begin to have marijuana meet federal guidelines for prescription drugs and be regulated by state-based programs to ensure safety.

Why these valuable trials are being undermined seems unconscionable. One University of Massachusetts at Amherst professor, Lyle E. Craker, has been trying for years to obtain a license to grow marijuana for medical research, only to be turned down by the DEA each time. Craker's goal is to try to develop a specific strain of marijuana to aid in the treatment of glaucoma. "It would be nice to be able to develop plant material that would be specific for glaucoma, specific to inhibit vomiting and all those other things that the plant is credited with doing. Currently, people with ailments are taking pot shots or they are going to illegal sources, which I suspect most of them are."[62]

This inability of labs to obtain marijuana for scientific testing leaves scientists in a strange catch-22. The federal government claims that marijuana has no value as a medicine, but if labs are prevented from testing and developing it, then marijuana can never be proven useful as a medicine. The few clinical trials that are being submitted for approval have found that marijuana could have significant benefits. For example, the CMCR at the University of California at San Diego sponsored several studies to assess whether marijuana is effective as a painkiller for HIV and multiple sclerosis patients who have suffered nerve damage. The studies proved marijuana had merit. Director Igor Grant says, "I was a little bit surprised, to tell the truth. . . . I somewhat expected that what we would get is a mixed result. . . . But the fact that all of them came up with a consistent result makes me feel a little more comfortable in saying we could have something here."[63]

The privately funded scientific laboratory Cannabis Science is trying to get FDA approval to begin clinical trials to develop numerous marijuana treatments. Some of these trials would involve the use of skin patches, tongue strips, and lozenges, which are all treatments that could give patients a consistent dosage of the active ingredients found in marijuana. As biology professor Bob Melamede states, "The key thing is we're addressing the government's concern that smoked marijuana is not medicine."[64] Melamede, Grant, and other scientists agree that marijuana medicines must be refined and delivery systems developed that could remove the objections to smoked marijuana. Andreas Rivera, the manager of Cannabis Therapeutics, a marijuana dispensary, states, "It's really about pain management instead of getting people super stoned."[65] Many scientists believe that the insistence on smoked marijuana has significantly harmed the fight for marijuana as effective medicine. "The current system of distribution may actually prevent cannabis from ever being accepted as a mainstream medicine by most patients and physicians,"[66] contends GW Pharmaceuticals spokesperson Mark Rogerson. GW Pharmaceuticals, located in Great Britain, has been responsible for developing the marijuana-derived drug Marinol. In the United States, however, the federal government is seriously hampering researchers' efforts to develop marijuana-based drugs.

> "The current system of distribution may actually prevent cannabis from ever being accepted as a mainstream medicine by most patients and physicians."[66]
>
> —GW Pharmaceuticals spokesperson Mark Rogerson.

Alcohol Is Far More Dangerous

The federal government's persistence in treating marijuana as a dangerous drug defies logic. Although alcohol accounts for roughly eighty thousand US deaths per year, the federal government does not classify alcohol as a controlled substance. Such a classification places marijuana on a par with heroin and LSD, yet other commonly used painkillers or painkiller derivatives, such as morphine, cocaine, PCP, and methamphetamine, are classified as schedule 2, meaning that they are commonly prescribed by doctors and have legitimate medical uses.

Not only does marijuana's designation harm the development of legitimate medicines, it is simply incorrect: schedule 1 drugs are classified as having no accepted medical use, but marijuana has proven that it is

The States Can Adequately Regulate Medical Marijuana

States have risen to the challenge of dealing with the demand for medical marijuana by passing laws that address the needs of their residents. In November 2012, Massachusetts became the eighteenth state (and DC) to permit its citizens to use medical marijuana. Other states have removed criminal penalties for possession of small amounts of marijuana for personal use under certain conditions.

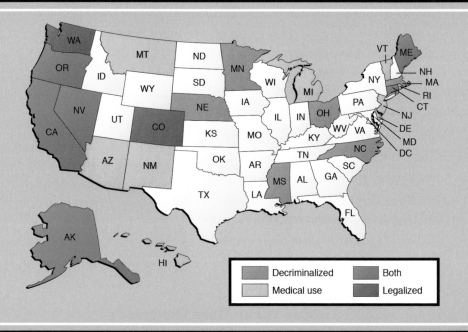

Legend:
- Decriminalized
- Medical use
- Both
- Legalized

Source: Marijuana Policy Project, National Organization for the Normalization of Marijuana Laws, 2012. www.mpp.org.

indeed useful as a medicine. Though much of the evidence is anecdotal, there is too much of it to ignore. Take the case of Scott Rozman, who had a rare form of cancer that was treated aggressively with chemotherapy. Rozman lost 60 pounds (27kg) in two months, and had such severe nausea that he could not eat. "The doctors thought I was a dead man,"[67] Rozman contends. His doctors prescribed marijuana, which improved his nausea so much that he was able to keep food down. It also calmed his anxiety and allowed him to face his illness without giving up. Incidents such as Rozman's have caused doctors such as Rob MacCoun, a psychologist and a professor of law and public policy at the University of California at Berkeley, to claim that "the statement 'it has no accepted medical use' is simply wrong as a statement of fact."[68]

Federal Drug Laws Create a Catch-22

The fact that the federal government can prosecute marijuana users and the physicians who prescribe or dispense the drug, even when they are in compliance with state law, is a problem. Wendy S. Goffe is an attorney in Seattle, Washington. She is worried that her clients may be prosecuted by the federal government in spite of having obtained prescriptions to use marijuana. She spent a day at a conference for lawyers seeking to understand Seattle's marijuana laws, only to come away with this thought:

> What I gleaned from this seminar is that until federal law changes, state regulation of any kind is simply lipstick on a pig. The current patchwork of state laws leaves dispensaries, producers and medical users unprotected. It leaves law enforcement officials confused about their obligations because any marijuana use or possession violates federal law. And of even greater concern, individuals engaged in legal activity under any state's law are still vulnerable to federal prosecution.[69]

Successful State Regulation Is Possible

Yet states persist in attempting to enact commonsense laws to govern medical marijuana in their states. Some are succeeding. Colorado, for example, is seen as a model for setting up medical marijuana as a business that does not flout federal laws. Dispensaries and distribution centers are watched twenty-four hours a day by security cameras linked to the Colorado Medical Marijuana Enforcement Division to ensure that no illegal activity goes on. At RiverRock, a medical marijuana dispensary, each marijuana plant—of which there are hundreds—is tagged with a radio frequency identification chip. Employees have to sign in each time they enter the inventory room. These rigorous standards are all part of a regulatory model created by Colorado state legislators. The system proves that states can self-regulate. Senator Pat Steadman, who was involved in Colorado's legalization process, explains: "We've recognized that this is a business, and our voters have said that they want patients to have access to this medicine. . . . We want to make sure there is a legitimate industry to serve this population, so we've created a tight chain of control from seed to sale."[70]

> "We've recognized that this is a business, and our voters have said that they want patients to have access to this medicine. . . . We want to make sure there is a legitimate industry to serve this population, so we've created a tight chain of control from seed to sale."[70]
>
> —Colorado senator Pat Steadman.

Colorado has become a model for other states that are learning from its experience. Connecticut, for example, has set up an even more tightly regulated system than Colorado's—again proving that states can and will successfully govern the drug. William Rubenstein, commissioner of Connecticut's Department of Consumer Protection, claims that "Connecticut's law has been called the most restrictive in the country, but I prefer to call it the best designed."[71] Under the law, Connecticut will license only ten indoor producers, and marijuana will only be sold from selected, stand-alone pharmacies specifically designed to sell not only smokable marijuana but also other delivery systems such as inhalers and patches. By keeping growing and distribution centers under tight control, Connecticut hopes to ensure that marijuana is purchased only for medical use.

Allowing states to govern medical marijuana circumvents federal objections while allowing patients to choose a successful treatment. It is a solution that satisfies everyone involved in the issue.

Source Notes

Overview: Medical Marijuana

1. Pew Research Center, "Public Support for Legalizing Medical Marijuana," April 1, 2010. www.people-press.org.
2. Gustin L. Reichbach, "A Judge's Plea for Pot," *New York Times*, May 16, 2012. www.nytimes.com.
3. Michael Scherer, "What Is President Obama's Problem with Medical Marijuana?," *Time*, May 3, 2012. http://swampland.time.com.
4. Quoted in Dylan Scott, "Medical Marijuana: Do States Know How to Regulate It?," *Governing*, August 2012. www.governing.com.
5. Quoted in McCarton Ackerman, "Obama Owns Up to a War on Weed," *Fix*, April 27, 2012. www.thefix.com.
6. Quoted in Scott, "Medical Marijuana: Do States Know How to Regulate It?"
7. Quoted in Scherer, "What Is President Obama's Problem with Medical Marijuana?"

Chapter One: Is Medical Marijuana Effective Medicine?

8. Marijuana Policy Project, "Effective Arguments for Medical Marijuana Advocates," January 2010. www.mpp.org.
9. Daniel Abrams et al., "Cannabis in Painful HIV-Associated Sensory Neuropathy: A Randomized Placebo-Controlled Trial," *Neurology*, 2007. www.cmcr.ucsd.edu.
10. Erin Hildebrandt, "Medical Marijuana: A Surprising Solution to Severe Morning Sickness," *Mothering*, May/June 2004. www.mothering.com.
11. Quoted in Marijuana Policy Project, "Let This Be the Year for Medical Marijuana." www.mpp.org.
12. Janet E. Joy et al., "Marijuana and Medicine: Assessing the Science Base," National Academy Press, March 1999. www.iom.edu.
13. Quoted in Sandra Bennett and William Bennett, "Pro-Drug Advocates Market Marijuana to State Legislatures: 'Medical' Marijuana Is a Hoax!," *Drug Watch World*, October 8, 2003. www.drugwatch.org.

14. National Eye Institute, "Glaucoma and Marijuana Use," June 21, 2005. www.nei.nih.gov.

15. Glaucoma Research Foundation, "Medical Marijuana," April 24, 2012. www.glaucoma.org.

16. American Academy of Pediatrics, "Marijuana and Glaucoma: Separating Fact from Fiction," EyeSmart. www.geteyesmart.org.

17. Joep Killestein, "Safety, Tolerability, and Efficacy of Orally Administered Cannabinoids in MS," *Neurology*, May 2002. www.neurology.org.

18. Anthony Feinstein, "Effects of Cannabis on Cognitive Function in Patients with Multiple Sclerosis," *Neurology*, March 2011. www.neurology.org.

19. Quoted in News Medical, "Endocannabinoids Found to Spread and Prolong Pain," August 13, 2009. www.news-medical.net.

20. Gregory Simon, "Ask the Doctor Q & A," Depression and Bipolar Support Alliance, January 2012. www.dbsalliance.org.

21. Quoted in Uncommon Knowledge, "Best of Quitter's Wisdom: 2." www.uncommonforum.com.

Chapter Two: Is Medical Marijuana Safe?

22. Marijuana Policy Project, "Effective Arguments for Medical Marijuana Advocates."

23. Ron Marczyk, "Worth Repeating," Toke of the Town, February 16, 2011. www.tokeofthetown.com.

24. Quoted in Maia Szalavitz, "Study: Smoking Marijuana Not Linked with Lung Damage," *Time*, January 10, 2012. http://healthland.time.com.

25. Quoted in Jennifer Lollar, "Marijuana Smoke Not as Damaging to Lungs as Cigarette Smoke," UAB News, January 10, 2012. www.uab.edu.

26. Mary Romeyn, *Nutrition and HIV: A New Model for Treatment.* San Francisco: Jossey-Bass, 1998, pp. 117–18.

27. Quoted in Maia Szalavitz, "Study: Marijuana Not Linked with Long Term Cognitive Impairment."

28. Office of National Drug Control Policy, "Marijuana." www.whitehouse.gov.

29. Quoted in Rachel Bracker, "Marijuana Use Possibly Linked to Specific Type of Testicular Cancer," *Daily Trojan*, September 11, 2010. http://dailytrojan.com.

30. R. Singh et al., "Evaluation of the DNA Damaging Potential of Cannabis Cigarette Smoke by the Determination of Acetaldehyde Derived N2-ethyl-2'-deoxyguanosine Adducts," PubMed, June 2009. www.ncbi.nlm.nih.gov.

31. Quoted in Ed Edelson, "Marijuana Use May Raise Risk of Heart Attack, Stroke," *Healthday News*, May 13, 2008. www.healthday.com.

32. Hanan El Marroun et al., "Intrauterine Cannabis Exposure Affects Fetal Growth Trajectories: The Generation R Study," *Journal of the American Academy of Child & Adolescent Psychiatry*, December 2009. www.jaacap.com.

33. Experience Project, "Severe Panic Attacks After Smoking Weed," July 1, 2009. www.experienceproject.com.

34. D.H. Linszen et al., "Cannabis Use and Age at Onset of Symptoms in Subjects at Clinical High Risk for Psychosis," *Acta Psychiatrica Scandinavica*, January 2012. www.ncbi.nlm.gov.

35. Joseph M. Pierre, "Cannabis, Synthetic Cannabinoids, and Psychosis Risk: What the Evidence Says," *Current Psychiatry*, September 2011. www.currentpsychiatry.com.

36. *Duke Today*, "Adolescent Pot Use Leaves Lasting Mental Deficits," August 27, 2012. http://today.duke.edu.

37. National Institute on Drug Abuse, "Marijuana," May 2010. www.drugabuse.gov.

Chapter Three: Should Medical Marijuana Be Legalized?

38. Lynn O'Connor, "Marijuana Addiction Today," *Psychology Today*, May 2012. www.psychologytoday.com.

39. Cassie Rodenberg, "Letter from a Marijuana Addict," *Scientific American*, April 30, 2012. www.scientificamerican.com.

40. Quoted in KQED, "Interview with Attorney Haag on Pot Operations: 'If It's Close to Children, That's a Line We're Going to Draw,'" March 15, 2012. www.kqed.org.

41. Associated Press, "Our View: California Pot Business Set Bad Example for Maine," *Portland (ME) Press Herald*, October 12, 2011. www.pressherald.com.

67

42. Quoted in KQED, "Interview with Attorney Haag on Pot Operations."

43. Quoted in Matthew Grant Anson, "Study Debunks Belief That Marijuana Dispensaries Cause Crime," *American News Report*, June 6, 2012. http://americannewsreport.com.

44. Jill Cooper, "Against Drugged Driving," *New York Times*, December 19, 2011. www.nytimes.com.

45. Jann Gumbiner, "Is Marijuana Addictive?," *Psychology Today*, December 5, 2010. www.psychologytoday.com.

46. Quoted in Rheana Murray, "Medical Pot Won't Push Teens to Light Up," *New York Daily News*, November 5, 2011. www.nydailynews.com.

47. ScienceDaily, "No Evidence Medical Marijuana Increases Teen Drug Use, Study Suggests," June 18, 2012. www.sciencedaily.com.

48. Quoted in Paul Armentano, "Study: Medical Cannabis Dispensaries Not Associated with Neighborhood Crime," *NORML Blog*, June 7, 2012. http://blog.norml.org.

49. Quoted in Armentano, "Study."

50. Mark Maginn, "Living with Pain: The Fed Crackdown on Medical Marijuana," American News Report, August 16, 2012. http://americannewsreport.com.

51. Paul Armentano, "Banning Weed Is Bad Medicine," *Los Angeles Times*, July 27, 2012. www.latimes.com.

52. Quoted in CU Newsroom, "Study Shows Medical Marijuana Laws Reduce Traffic Deaths," November 29, 2011. www.ucdenver.edu.

53. Joseph D. McNamara, "The Law Adds to the Harm," *New York Times*, December 19, 2011. www.nytimes.com.

Chapter Four: Can States Adequately Regulate Medical Marijuana?

54. Quoted in John Hoeffel, "U.S. Decrees That Marijuana Has No Accepted Medical Use," *Los Angeles Times*, July 9, 2011. www.latimes.com.

55. Quoted in Anna Wilde Mathews, "Is Marijuana Medicine?," *Wall Street Journal*, January 18, 2010. www.wsj.com.

56. Quoted in Norimitsu Onishi, "Cities Balk as Federal Law on Marijuana Is Enforced," *New York Times*, June 30, 2012. www.nytimes.com.

57. Quoted in *PBS NewsHour*, "California Raids Threaten Medical Marijuana Regulation," November 8, 2011. www.pbs.org.

58. *Los Angeles Times*, "Hazy Marijuana Laws," April 5, 2012. www.latimes.com.

59. Quoted in Michigan Radio Newsroom, "Stateside: That Status of Michigan's Medical Marijuana Law," October 31, 2012. www.michiganradio.org.

60. Quoted in Devlin Barrett, "Attorney General Signals Shift in Marijuana Policy," Associated Press, March 18, 2009. www.ap.org.

61. Quoted in Jann S. Wenner, "Ready for the Fight: *Rolling Stone* Interview with Barack Obama," *Rolling Stone*, May 10, 2012. www.rollingstone.com.

62. Quoted in Robert Rizzuto, "DEA Rejects UMass Professor Lyle Craker's Bid to Grow Marijuana for Federally-Regulated Medical Research," *Springfield (MA) Republican*, August 25, 2011. www.masslive.com.

63. Quoted in John Ingold, "Medical-Marijuana Advocates Seek Society's Approval," *Denver Post*, July 4, 2010. www.denverpost.com.

64. Quoted in Ingold, "Medical-Marijuana Advocates Seek Society's Approval."

65. Quoted in Ingold, "Medical-Marijuana Advocates Seek Society's Approval."

66. Quoted in Ingold, "Medical-Marijuana Advocates Seek Society's Approval."

67. Quoted in Courtney Hutchison, "Marijuana Advocates Sue Feds After DEA Rejects Weed as Medicine," ABC News, July 12, 2011. http://abcnews.go.com.

68. Quoted in Hutchison, "Marijuana Advocates Sue Feds After DEA Rejects Weed as Medicine."

69. Wendy S. Goffe, "On Medical Marijuana, Federal Law Leaves States in Purple Haze," *Forbes*, September 12, 2012. www.forbes.com.

70. Quoted in Dylan Scott, "Medical Marijuana."

71. Quoted in Judy Benson, "Marijuana Now Legal for Medical Use in Connecticut," *Day*, October 2, 2012. www.theday.com.

Medical Marijuana Facts

Attitudes Toward Medical Marijuana

- An October 2011 ABC/*Washington Post* poll found that 81 percent of Americans think doctors should be able to prescribe medical marijuana to patients with certain medical conditions.
- Support for legalizing marijuana doubled between 1996 and 2011, when 50 percent of those polled supported legalization for both recreational and medical use.
- According to 2010 data from the Substance Abuse and Mental Health Services Administration, more than 17 million Americans polled had used marijuana in the past month.
- Religious organizations that publicly support legalizing medical marijuana include the United Methodist Church, the Presbyterian Church, the Episcopal Church, the Unitarian Universalist Association, and the United Church of Christ.
- According to the marijuana advocacy group NORML, 750,000 to 1.1 million medical marijuana users lived in California in 2011.
- The second-largest physician group in the country, the American College of Physicians, advocates a reclassification of marijuana under federal law to reflect its position that the drug is a safe and effective medicine.

Uses for Medical Marijuana

- Animal studies have demonstrated that marijuana may inhibit cancerous tumor growth by blocking the growth of blood vessels that are necessary for tumors to develop.
- Experiments using a cannabis-based extract sprayed under the tongue demonstrated that cannabis may improve sleep quality.
- Hepatitis C patients who use marijuana are more likely to finish their medication regime, leading to a 300 percent increase in successful treatment.
- Ongoing clinical studies suggest that marijuana might help lower blood pressure in people with hypertension by dilating the blood vessels, improving sleep, and reducing anxiety.

- A 2008 clinical study found that marijuana has antibacterial properties that can help stop the spread of MRSA, a drug-resistant staph bacterium that causes around twenty thousand hospital deaths annually.

Cannabis-Based Prescription Drugs

- Savitex, a cannabis-based drug that has been approved in Canada and other countries, is used by thousands of patients to treat pain and other conditions; clinical trials of the drug are currently under way in the United States.
- A number of clinical studies and patient reports state that while Marinol, a synthetic THC preparation, effectively mitigates pain, users may experience many unwanted side effects, including dizziness and abnormal thinking.
- Whereas Marinol is synthetic, Savitex uses plant-based ingredients, which researchers believe mitigates the unwanted psychoactive side effects of Marinol and make it a more effective pain treatment.
- Marinol may cause withdrawal symptoms that include diarrhea, hot flashes, restlessness, insomnia, and irritability.

Medical Marijuana and Mental Health

- According to an assessment of existing research by Stanley Zammit at Cardiff University in Wales, many of the studies that link marijuana use and depression did not assess symptoms of depression before marijuana use, making the results invalid.
- According to Danish researcher Mikkel Arendt, patients treated for cannabis-induced schizophrenia would have developed the disorder even if they had never used marijuana.
- Columbia University's National Center on Addiction and Substance Abuse reported in 2011 that teens who used marijuana at least once in the past month are twenty-six times more likely to use other drugs than are teens who have never smoked marijuana.
- Several studies have reported that marijuana use narrows arteries in the brain, which can restrict blood flow and lead to impaired learning and attention problems.
- Research by Daniele Piomelli of the University of California at Irvine in 2012 demonstrated that substances found in marijuana significantly reduced the symptoms of schizophrenia without the side effects typical of antipsychotic drugs, including weight gain and diabetes.

Related Organizations and Websites

American Alliance for Medical Cannabis (AAMC)
44500 Tide Ave.
Arch Cape, OR 97102
phone: (503) 436-1882
e-mail: contact@letfreedomgrow.com • website: www.letfreedomgrow.com

The AAMC is an advocacy group that is dedicated to promoting the rights of medical marijuana patients. The AAMC provides information on the most common medical uses of marijuana and works to educate patients and caregivers so that they may make informed decisions when using marijuana to treat medical conditions.

Americans for Safe Access (ASA)
1322 Webster St., Suite 402
Oakland, CA 94612
phone: (510) 251-1856
e-mail: info@safeaccessnow.org • website: www.safeaccessnow.org

ASA is an organization of patients, doctors, scientists, and others concerned with ensuring access to marijuana for medical use and research. To this end, ASA promotes legislation, education, and grassroots activism that support the safe and legal access for patients and their caregivers.

Center for Medicinal Cannabis Research (CMCR)
220 Dickinson St., Suite B
San Diego, CA 92103
phone: (619) 543-5024
e-mail: cmcr@ucsd.edu • website: www.cmcr.ucsd.edu

Established at the University of California at San Diego, the CMCR conducts research, including human studies, on the safety and efficacy of medical marijuana. The center's published research is described on its website along with additional educational resources. The CMCR supports cannabis research throughout the state of California.

Drug Free America Foundation, Inc. (DFAF)
5999 Central Ave., Suite 301
Saint Petersburg, FL 33710
phone: (727) 828-0211
website: www.dfaf.org

The DFAF is a drug-prevention organization that develops and promotes policies and legislation that will reduce illegal drug use and the problems associated with it. The foundation opposes the decriminalization or legalization of any illicit drug, including marijuana for medical use.

Drug Policy Alliance (DPA)
70 W. Thirty-Sixth St., Sixteenth Floor
New York, NY 10018
phone: (212) 613-8020
e-mail: nyc@drugpolicy.org • website: www.drugpolicy.org

The DPA supports alternatives to the current drug policy in the United States and state initiatives that would render marijuana legal and accessible to patients and their caregivers. The alliance publishes position papers, research briefs, and fact sheets to educate both citizens and policy makers.

Drug Watch International
PO Box 45218
Omaha, NE 68145
phone: (402) 384-9212
website: www.drugwatch.org

Drug Watch International is a nonprofit organization that promotes strategies to create a drug-free world. The group opposes the legalization of all illicit drugs. To this end, Drug Watch International supports the expansion of drug education and prevention programs as well as law enforcement strategies aimed at reducing drug use and trafficking.

Marijuana Policy Project (MMP)
236 Massachusetts Ave. NE, Suite 400
Washington, DC 20002
phone: (202) 462-5747
e-mail: info@mpp.org • website: www.mpp.org

The MMP advocates the responsible use of marijuana for both medical and nonmedical use. The group works to increase public awareness about marijuana and to reform current state and federal legislation that prohibits its use.

National Center on Addiction and Substance Abuse (CASA)
Columbia University
633 Third Ave., Nineteenth Floor
New York, NY 10017
phone: (212) 841-5200
website: www.casacolumbia.org

CASA is a science-based organization that seeks to educate the general public about the dangers of illicit drug abuse and the disease of addiction. The center publishes a variety of research-based papers that detail the problems associated with addiction and effective ways to help users lead drug-free lives.

National Institute on Drug Abuse (NIDA)
National Institutes of Health
6001 Executive Blvd., Room 5213
Bethesda, MD 20892
phone: (301) 443-1124
e-mail: information@nida.nih.gov • website: www.nida.nih.gov

NIDA is a division of the National Institutes of Health, which is part of the US Department of Health and Human Services. NIDA both sponsors and conducts research on drug abuse and addiction in order to improve prevention and treatment efforts. It publishes a variety of educational materials, including research reports, fact sheets, and select publications on marijuana.

National Organization for the Reform of Marijuana Laws (NORML)
1600 K St. NW, Suite 501
Washington, DC 20006
phone: (202) 483-5500
e-mail: norml@norml.org • website: www.norml.org

NORML is a marijuana advocacy group that works to increase public support for the end of marijuana prohibition for both medical and recreational use. The organization lobbies for marijuana policy reform at both the state and federal levels. It publishes numerous educational materials on its website.

For Further Research

Books

Greg Campbell, *Pot, Inc.: Inside Medical Marijuana, America's Most Outlaw Industry*. New York: Sterling, 2012.

Jonathan P. Caulkins et al., *Marijuana Legalization: What Everyone Needs to Know*. New York: Oxford University Press, 2012.

John Geluardi, *Cannabiz: The Explosive Rise of the Medical Marijuana Industry*. Sausalito, CA: PoliPointPress, 2010.

Julie Holland, ed., *The Pot Book: A Complete Guide to Cannabis: Its Role in Medicine, Politics, Science, and Culture*. Rochester, VT: Park Street, 2010.

Michael Kuhar, *The Addicted Brain: Why We Abuse Drugs, Alcohol, and Nicotine*. Upper Saddle River, NJ: Financial Times, 2011.

Mickey Martin, Ed Rosenthal, and Gregory T. Carter, *Medical Marijuana 101*. Oakland, CA: Quick American Archives, 2012.

Trish Regan, *Joint Ventures: Inside America's Almost Legal Marijuana Industry*. Hoboken, NJ: John Wiley & Sons, 2011.

Robin Room et al., *Cannabis Policy: Moving Beyond Stalemate*. New York: Oxford University Press, 2010.

Periodicals

Hal Arkowitz and Scott O. Lilienfeld, "Experts Tell the Truth About Pot," *Scientific American*, February 22, 2012.

Seth Cline, "Where and How Can You Smoke Pot Legally Now?," *U.S. News & World Report*, November 9, 2012.

Dinah Miller and Annette Hanson, "Medical Marijuana Laws Make a Farce of Medicine," *Baltimore Sun*, March 7, 2012.

Dan Murphy, "On Marijuana and the Mexican Drug War," *Christian Science Monitor*, November 8, 2012.

New York Times, "Marijuana and Medical Marijuana," November 8, 2012.

Amanda Reiman, "Marijuana: A Failure to Regulate, but Not by Dispensaries," *Los Angeles Times*, October 2, 2012.

Daniel B. Wood, "Confusion Reigns over Medical Marijuana as States and Feds Clash," *Christian Science Monitor*, December 13, 2011.

Internet Sources

Chelsea Conaboy, "Massachusetts Voters Approve Ballot Measure to Legalize Medical Marijuana," Boston.com, November 6, 2012. http://boston.com.

Kathleen Doheny, "Marijuana Relieves Chronic Pain, Research Shows," WebMD, August 30, 2010. www.webmd.com.

Charles Giannasio, "Marijuana Is Addictive, Destructive and Dangerous," CNBC, April 20, 2010. www.cnbc.com.

Huffington Post, "Marijuana Businesses Expected to Boom After Colorado, Washington Pot Legalization," November 7, 2012. www.huffingtonpost.com.

Martin A. Lee, "Victory for Pot Means Beginning of the End of Our Crazy Drug War," *Daily Beast*, November 8, 2012. www.thedailybeast.com.

Reuters, "Pot Smoking During Pregnancy May Stunt Fetal Growth," January 22, 2010. www.reuters.com.

John Suthers, "Commentary: Medical Marijuana a Threat to State's Children," *EdNews Voices* (blog), February 6, 2012. www.ednewscolorado.org

Index

*Note: Boldface page numbers
indicate illustrations.*

Abrams, Daniel, 15
addiction, to marijuana
   is a risk, 41
   is unlikely, 47
adolescents
   impact of marijuana use on, 36, 38
   legalized medical marijuana and
      increased use by, 43, 47–48
American Academy of Pediatrics, 22–23
American Medical Association (AMA), 17,
   19
Anderson, D. Mark, 51
anxiety/panic, 24–25, 32, 36, 70
appetite stimulation, 14, 15, 17
Arbelaez, Norton, 10
Armentano, Paul, 50

brain
   impact of marijuana on, 34
   structures of, functions of/effects of
      marijuana on, **16**
British Medical Journal, 45

cancer, 34–35
   marijuana as treatment for side effects of
      chemotherapy, 6–7
cannabinoids, 14, 24
Center for Medicinal Cannabis Research
   (CMCR), 14–15, 18, 60
Centers for Disease Control and Prevention
   (CDC), 30
Centre for Mental Health Research
   (Australian National University), 32
Choo, Esther, 48
Colorado Department of Health, 43–44
controlled substances, federal classification
   of, **21**
Cooper, Jill, 45
Cortessis, Victoria, 35

Craker, Lyle E., 60
crime
   legalized medical marijuana would not
      increase, 48–50
   marijuana dispensaries contribute to,
      44

DeAngelo, Steve, 11
death(s)
   dose of marijuana necessary to produce,
      28
   due to alcohol, 61
   leading causes of, **30**
Department of Justice, US, 10
depression, 24–25
dispensaries
   crime and, 44
   difficulty in regulating, 54–56
   have negative impacts on communities,
      56
driving, under influence of marijuana
   is dangerous, 44–45
   risks of, are overblown, 50–51
Drug Enforcement Administration, US
   (DEA), 53–54
drugs
   abused/misused, number of emergency
      department visits attributable to, **37**
   federal classification of, **21**
   number of cases of abuse/dependence
      on, by drug, **42**
DuPont, Robert, 22

emergency department, number of visits
   attributable to drug abuse/misuse, by
   drug, **37**
endocannabinoids/endocannabinoid
   system, 14, 24

federal government
   clash between state laws on medical
      marijuana and, 8, 57, 63

classification of controlled substances by, **21**
marijuana research is impeded by, 59–61
position on medical marijuana, 7–8, 10–11, 57–58
Feinstein, Anthony, 23
Food and Drug Administration (FDA), 19–20, 33

Gable, Robert, 27, 28–29
Garcon, George, 11
glaucoma, 22–23, 57, 60
Glaucoma Research Foundation, 22
Goffe, Wendy S., 63
Granger, Christopher, 35
Grant, Igor, 60, 61
Gumbiner, Jann, 47

Haag, Melinda, 42–43, 44
Hildebrandt, Erin, 17
HIV disease, 31
Holder, Eric, 57–58

Internal Revenue Service (IRS), 10–11

Jones, Rick, 57
Journal of Drug Policy Analysis, 43
Journal of the American Academy of Child & Adolescent Psychiatry, 35, 43
Journal of the American Medical Association, 29

Kerlikowske, R. Gil, 40
Kertesz, Stefan, 29, 31
Killestein, Joep, 23

legalization, of medical marijuana
argument against, 40–45
argument for, 46–51
debate over, 39
Leonhart, Michele M., 54
Linszen, D.H., 36, 38
Los Angeles Times (newspaper), 56, 57
lung function/ disorders, 29, 31, 34

MacCoun, Rob, 63
Maginn, Mark, 49
Marczyk, Ron, 28

marijuana
addiction to, 41, 47
chemicals in, 14
concerns about mental health and, 36, 38
effects on user, by associated brain structure, **16**
as gateway drug, 40, 46–47
impact on adolescents, 36, 38
number of emergency department visits attributable to, **37**
states' policies on, **62**
See also medical marijuana
Marijuana Policy Project, 14, 15
on safety of marijuana, 13, 27–28, 29
on state regulation of medical marijuana, 59
Marijuana Resource Center, 33
McNamara, Joseph D., 51
medical marijuana
cancer and, 34–35
cardiovascular/reproductive issues and, 35
clash between federal and state laws on, 8, 57, 63
debate over effectiveness of, 12
debate over legalization of, 39
debate over safety of, 26
debate over states' ability to adequately regulate, 52
in depression, 24–25
federal position on, 7–8, 10–11, 57–58
in glaucoma, 22–23, 57, 60
lung disorders and, 29–31, 34
for nausea/appetite stimulation, 15, 17, 31
in pain relief, 14–15, 23–24, 31
public support for, 6, **49**, 56
regulation of, in states allowing, 8–10
for seizures/spasticity, 17–18, 23
side effects of, 31–32
Meier, Madeline, 38
Melamede, Bob, 61
multiple sclerosis (MS), 17–18, 23

National Eye Institute, 22
National Institute on Drug Abuse (NIDA), 20, 35, 40

on marijuana as medicine, 38
Neugebauer, Volker, 24
Neurology (journal), 15, 23
New York Times (newspaper), 6
Nutrition and HIV (Romeyn), 31

Obama, Barack, 10, 58
O'Connor, Lynn, 41
Office of National Drug Control Policy
    (ONDCP), 19, 34
opinion polls, on support for medical
    marijuana, 6

pain, 14–15, 23–24, 31
panic. *See* anxiety/panic
Pettit, Andrew, 44
Pew Research, 6, **49**
Pierre, Joseph M., 36
Pletcher, Mark, 29, 32
Psychology Today (magazine), 41
psychosis, risk from marijuana use, 32, 33,
    36, 38

Rand Corporation, 49
Rees, Daniel I., 48, 50–51
Reichbach, Gustin L., 6–7
Rivera, Andreas, 61
Rodenberg, Cassie, 41
Rogerson, Mark, 61
Rolling Stone (magazine), 10
Romeyn, Mary, 31

Rozman, Scott, 15, 17, 62–63
Rubenstein, William, 64
Russoniello, Joseph, 55, 56

Sagen, Thea, 54
Scherer, Michael, 8
schizophrenia, 32, 36, 71
Simon, Gregory, 24, 25
spasticity, 17–18, 23
state(s)
    can adequately regulate medical
        marijuana, 59–64
    cannot adequately regulate medical
        marijuana, 53–58
    debate over ability to adequately regulate
        medical marijuana, 52
    policies on marijuana by, **62**
Steadman, Pat, 64
surveys, on support for medical marijuana,
    6, **49**, 56

Tait, Robert, 32
tetrahydrocannabinal (THC), 14, 15, 28
    effects on user, by associated brain
        structure, **16**
    marijuana treatment admissions and
        levels of, **55**

vaporization, 31

Wagner, Benjamin B., 54–55